ISBN 978-1-334-97905-7
PIBN 10601246

1 MONTH OF
FREE
READING

at
www.ForgottenBooks.com

By purchasing this book you are eligible for one month membership to ForgottenBooks.com, giving you unlimited access to our entire collection of over 700,000 titles via our web site and mobile apps.

To claim your free month visit:
www.forgottenbooks.com/free601246

English
Français
Deutsche
Italiano
Español
Português

www.forgottenbooks.com

Mythology Photography **Fiction**
Fishing Christianity **Art** Cooking
Essays Buddhism Freemasonry
Medicine **Biology** Music **Ancient**
Egypt Evolution Carpentry Physics
Dance Geology **Mathematics** Fitness
Shakespeare **Folklore** Yoga Marketing
Confidence Immortality Biographies
Poetry **Psychology** Witchcraft
Electronics Chemistry History **Law**
Accounting **Philosophy** Anthropology
Alchemy Drama Quantum Mechanics
Atheism Sexual Health **Ancient History**
Entrepreneurship Languages Sport
Paleontology Needlework Islam
Metaphysics Investment Archaeology
Parenting Statistics Criminology
Motivational

INVESTIGATION OF CONCENTRATION OF ECONOMIC POWER

TEMPORARY NATIONAL ECONOMIC COMMITTEE

A STUDY MADE FOR THE TEMPORARY NATIONAL ECONOMIC COMMITTEE, SEVENTY-SIXTH CONGRESS, THIRD SESSION, PURSUANT TO PUBLIC RESOLUTION NO. 113 (SEVENTY-FIFTH CONGRESS) AUTHORIZING AND DIRECTING A SELECT COMMITTEE TO MAKE A FULL AND COMPLETE STUDY AND INVESTIGATION WITH RESPECT TO THE CONCENTRATION OF ECONOMIC POWER IN, AND FINANCIAL CONTROL OVER, PRODUCTION AND DISTRIBUTION OF GOODS AND SERVICES

MONOGRAPH No. 43

THE MOTION PICTURE INDUSTRY— A PATTERN OF CONTROL

Printed for the use of the
Temporary National Economic Committee

UNITED STATES
GOVERNMENT PRINTING OFFICE
WASHINGTON : 1941

II

ACKNOWLEDGMENT

This monograph was written by

DANIEL BERTRAND
Administrative Assistant, Temporary National Economic Committee

W. DUANE EVANS
Senior Economist, Bureau of Labor Statistics, United States Department of Labor

E. L. BLANCHARD
Member, Temporary National Economic Committee Staff

The Temporary National Economic Committee is greatly indebted to these authors for their contribution to the literature of the subject under review.

The status of the materials in the volume is precisely the same as that of other carefully prepared testimony when given by individual witnesses; it is information submitted for committee deliberation. No matter what the official capacity of the witness or author may be, the publication of his testimony, report, or monograph by the committee in no way signifies nor implies assent to, or approval of, any of the facts, opinion, or recommendations, nor acceptance thereof in whole or in part by the members of the Temporary National Economic Committee, individually or collectively. Sole and undivided responsibility for every statement in such testimony, report, or monographs rests entirely upon the respective authors.

(Signed)   JOSEPH C. O'MAHONEY,
Chairman, Temporary National Economic Committee.

TABLE OF CONTENTS

TABLES

LETTER OF TRANSMITTAL

Hon. JOSEPH C. O'MAHONEY,
Chairman, Temporary National Economic Committee,
United States Senate, Washington, D. C.

MY DEAR SENATOR: The monograph, The Motion Picture Industry—A Pattern of Control, is submitted for the information of the
Committee. It was prepared by Mr. Duane Evans, senior economist
in the Department of Labor, Mr. Daniel Bertrand, administrative
assistant to the executive secretary of the Temporary National
Economic Committee, and Miss Edna Blanchard, member of the
T. N. E. C. staff. The Department of Labor generously detailed
Mr. Evans temporarily to the Committee to assist in the preparation
of this report. The study grew out of the continued interest in the
economic problems of the industry of Mr. Evans and Mr. Bertrand
since the N. R. A. period, when both were connected with the administration of the code of fair competition for the motion picture industry.

This study gives a concise treatment of the economic development
of the motion picture industry and the problems raised by its rapid
growth and its present domination by a few large companies. It is of
particular importance in the studies of the concentration of economic
power for the span of time involved is so short, and the events so recent,
that the pattern of control can be kept constantly before the reader.
Thus, the monograph offers evidence of the ways in which great aggre-
gates of economic power are created and the methods used in their operation. The struggle for dominance goes forward ruthlessly, with
ofttimes little regard for the motion picture industry's social responsi-
bilities. Finally, as power has become lodged in a few hands, it has
become necessary for the Department of Justice to take steps to protect
the public interest. After prolonged discussion and litigation a consent decree has been entered into between that Department and the
industry. This decree is analyzed in the present report, together with
certain observations as to its effect on the problems which it seeks
to solve.

The authors have been careful to present a factual description of
the motion picture industry as an important economic structure. They
do not moralize, nor make judgments concerning the events, good and
bad, which they describe. Conclusions are not recommendations but
summaries of the facts. The monograph, therefore, serves a very
useful purpose in its collection and condensation of data on the
motion picture industry. It should be of inestimable value to the
congressional committees vested with the duty of reviewing proposed
legislation which occurs each year.

Respectfully submitted.

THEODORE J. KREPS,
Economic Adviser.

INTRODUCTION

An outstanding lesson of history is that security, political or economic, is perhaps best achieved through organization and coordinated activity. The early economic theorists postulated numerous small units struggling with each other under a rule of "free competition" which required that those least fitted for the conflict, the "sub-marginal establishments," should inevitably be the losers. This is not coincidence, since these conditions characterized the more primitive forms of business organization. But just as individuals learned that there was safety in numbers, so business units learned there was safety in size, and today economists must concern themselves with the consequences of combination as well as those of competition.

In the United States at the end of the last century there was a rush to form huge combines. In the process of formation of these "trusts," huge business units sometimes clashed in economic warfare, with still greater power the prize for the victor and absorption the consequence to the vanquished.

In these battles of giants the consumer was in the position of innocent bystander. During the warfare he frequently benefited, but when the struggle ended the victor usually turned to him and demanded tribute in the form of higher prices. Sometimes the conflict was ended or avoided by agreement; the result to the consumer was the same.

When free competition prevailed, the consumer was the final arbiter, the referee. After combination had run its course and a monopoly or near monopoly was achieved, he lost this power. Once strong and now weak, he could defend himself only collectively, through the Government as his representative. The "trust-busting" campaigns of the early 1900's, the Sherman Act and the Clayton Act, all were efforts on the part of the Government to restore to the consumer a measure of the protection which had previously been afforded him by competition.

These legislative efforts were designed to break up the existing giant combines and prevent the formation of new ones. They did not, however, strike at the cause of formation of these combines. Size still conferred an advantage in the business struggle. The process of dog-eat-dog was permitted to continue, but was halted one step short of completion. The complex of economic forces brought about combination of business units into fewer and larger entities, but the rules laid down by Government prevented ultimate combination into a single industrial giant completely monopolizing one line of human activity. Industry after industry then fell into a common and familiar pattern. Instead of the multitude of individually small establishments visioned by the classical economist, the end product was an industry dominated by a few large closely-organized corporations.[1]

Denied the prize of an ultimate monopoly, these industrial leaders sought for "the next best thing."

It was early discovered that price competition was no longer desirable from the standpoint of these large companies. Price cuts were necessarily met by competitors, so no permanent advantage in the form of a larger share of the market was likely to result. The only inevitable consequence was that the profits of all concerned would be reduced. Price warfare was then seldom resorted to unless a specific end, with reasonable surety of its attainment, was in view.[2] Business had now achieved the moral level of diplomacy.

Out of the realization that some forms of competition were mutually disadvantageous was born a new era for business, symbolized by a new watchword and battle cry. It is heard on every side, and it is "cooperation."

Cooperation extends further than a recognition that price-cutting gives no lasting advantage to the person instituting it. It extends to preservation of the status-quo—the system under which the consumer, no longer protected by constant competition in the matter of prices, can be made to pay for all this industrial goodwill. Cooperation is then seldom a positive force; it is generally aimed at preventing change. Certain positive services may result. An example is the reporting and publishing of prices which is done by many trade associations. But here the objective is less to provide the consumer with a guide than it is to prevent the uninitiated or uninformed from thoughtlessly quoting prices below the going level.

Less openly, cooperation frequently takes forms which are designed to prevent the intrusion of new competitors into the business or industrial field. Consequently, there has grown up in a number of industries a more or less clear-cut distinction between the major interests, those large companies who virtually control and manage the affairs of the industry for their mutual benefit, and the independents (or outsiders). This has come about through the fear that the smaller enterprises, in their attempts to capture a larger portion of the business and so gain admittance to the inner circle, might in some way disturb a situation deemed satisfactory by the controlling interests.

The picture drawn above is not an uncommon one. It gives a rough outline of the development of the motion picture industry. In its case some of the steps are clearer, since the motion picture industry is in many ways a youngster among its industrial cousins. Accordingly, in the space of a relatively few years it has changed from an activity in the hands of a large number of small and financially weak individuals to an industry controlled by a few large companies which dominate its policies and control its actions.

---

[1] For an indication of the extent to which combination has been carried in American enterprise, cf. Temporary National Economic Committee, Monograph 27, "Structure of Industry," Part V, "Concentration of Production in Manufacturing," Walter F. Crowder, 1940.

[2] Cf the action of the R. J. Reynolds Tobacco Co. in reducing the listed wholesale price of Camel cigarettes from $6.45 to $6 per thousand in April 1928, reported in the trade press to be the result of Reynolds' determination to force another cigarette manufacturer to stop giving especially large discounts to mass buyers. (United Tobacco Journal, April 28, 1928, p. 7, and Printers' Ink, May 3, 1928, p. 182.) The price cut was rescinded by an increase to $6.40 per thousand in October 1929

CHAPTER I

THE PATTERN

CHAPTER I

THE PATTERN

DEVELOPMENT OF THE PATTERN [3]

The motion picture industry had its inception near the beginning of the present century as a "peep show" form of entertainment confined to backrooms and unused shops in a few large cities. Immediately popular and showing promise of large profits, it attracted the attention of entrepreneurs, speculators, investors, and other mid-wives of business. With their not wholly disinterested assistance, the infant industry was born.

As it grew up, it donned the outworn vestments of its not always respectable older cousins—vaudeville and the legitimate stage—by moving into closed or abandoned theaters formerly devoted to these types of entertainment. But, lusty and vital, the infant soon outgrew these hand-me-downs, and in 1914 it made its first appearance on Broadway in a theater built exclusively for showing motion pictures.

Today in the billion-dollar class, the industry has passed through a whirlwind development—rapid and successful. The meteoric rise and fall of personalities connected with the industry have been as vivid as any celluloid romance. Beginning as a flickering novelty, the motion picture today lives, tells a story, dispenses news, and even teaches in our schools. Once silent, it now sings, and the grey and jerky images of its early days have been steadied and given color.

From its beginning the industry has been characterized by some form of domination. It started in the hands of three companies—Edison, Biograph, and Vitagraph—who owned the principal patents covering the manufacture of equipment and film. These companies at first derived their profits more from the sale of equipment than from the sale of films.

The early motion picture films were produced on small budgets; they were short and could be exhibited in a few minutes. Audience turnover was rapid. The subject matter of these films was usually trivial—prize fights, dancers, incidents on park benches, and the like. Prints were sold outright, and their value depended principally on their novelty.

As the popularity of this form of entertainment spread, increased production became necessary to meet the public demand. A great many small producers and film distributors entered the field, but these newcomers at first constituted no immediate threat to the controlling interests.

At this time a fundamental change in the business methods of the industry took place. As matters stood, films lost value to an exhibitor

---

[3] The following sources have been freely consulted, in the preparation of this section: Lewis Jacobs, "The Rise of the American Film," Harcourt, Brace & Co., New York, 1939; Howard T. Lewis, "The Motion Picture Industry," D. Van Nostrand Co., Inc., New York, 1933; Terry Ramsaye, "A Million and One Nights", Simon & Schuster, New York, 1926; National Recovery Administration, "The Motion Picture Industry Study," Work Materials No. 34, 1936.

as their novelty was exhausted, so exhibitors traded films with each other. It was soon realized that the owner of a stock of films could make a profit by renting a single print to a number of exhibitors in succession, ·thus relieving these exhibitors from the necessity of making a cash investment in films. Consequently, the original method of outright sale of films to exhibitors was replaced by a licensing system. Under this system, title to the film remained with exchange men, and each film was licensed to various exhibitors until the print was no longer usable. This method of film distribution is still in use today.

In 1908, mainly to escape the effects of a patent war conducted chiefly by the Edison companies which held basic camera and projection equipment patents, the 10 leading interests in the industry organized the first trust—the Motion Picture Patents Co.[4] All patent interests and rights were pooled, and the cooperating companies were licensed to manufacture and lease motion pictures. The Eastman Kodak Co. cooperated by refusing to supply raw film to nonlicensed manufacturers. Films produced by the "patents pool" were handled by licensed exchange men who agreed to sell only to theaters with licensed projectors, and the exhibitors were required to pay for the right to use projectors in addition to film rentals. Through this system of licensing, the pool attempted control of the entire industry.

Resentment from those outside the "trust" took the form of bootlegging of films and projectors; protective organizations were formed and these organizations in turn prospered. Even licensed exchanges violated their contracts.

To check this adverse trend, the patents pool in 1910 organized 57 of the 58 exchanges then in existence into the General Film Co. to distribute the films of the 10 producers on a national scale. These licensed exchanges agreed to buy only "trust" pictures.

Despite the attempt to monopolize production and control distribution, the independent companies multiplied, flourished, and continned making pictures. By 1912 dozens of new producers and distributors, led by William Fox, operator of the fifty-eighth exchange, were offering the trust keen opposition. In this year a lawsuit was instituted against the trust as an unlawful conspiracy in restraint of trade. With antitrust sentiment sweeping the country, the General Film Co. was dissolved by the Federal courts in 1915. In 1917, the United States Supreme Court held, after years of hearings, that the patents company could not enforce exclusive use of licensed film on patented projectors in theaters, and the trust was declared legally dead.

Concomitant with the fight over patent rights was the controversy between short and the newly introduced feature-length films. The trust, interested primarily in quick and inexpensive production, greeted feature-length films with distaste and refused to distribute them. The independent companies, encouraged by the trust's reactionary policy, produced full-length features and sold exhibition rights to individual distributors each representing one or more States. These exchange men became known as "States' rights distributors." They were so successful that in 1914 a number of them joined with a

[4] Edison, Biograph, Vitagraph, Essanay, Selig, Lubin, and Kalem, domestic manufacturers; Melies and Pathe, French companies; and George Kleine, distributor.

few independent exhibitors to form the Paramount Pictures Corporation, which financed and distributed feature-length pictures produced by affiliated independent studios. This organization assured exhibitors a steady supply of features and the studios a steady market for their product.

The war years saw rapid growth of the industry. In 1914 America supplied half of the world movie production; by 1917 nearly all the world's motion pictures were produced in the United States. Increased profits, increased costs, and expansion in every direction were part of the war boom. Competition became more ruthless. Old corporations gave way to new ones. The industry had assumed the proportions of a large-scale operation depending on a mass market.

Up to this time exhibitors had been interested primarily in having a regular supply of new reels regardless of quality. The introduction of the feature picture and the star system made quality a more important factor, and the production of more pretentious films was expanded.

A new problem arose to engage the attention of producers. Theaters were numerous and widely scattered throughout the nation, and producers had to rely on distributors for efficient distribution of their product. But, since distributors handled the product of many producers, the individual producer found himself at the mercy of the distributor. With the recognition that full exploitation of their films could be accomplished only through securing control of distribution, the producers established affiliations for that purpose (see appendix I). This period as well as the early years after the war can indeed be described as one of large-scale economic warfare between powerful organizations for control of the industry.

During the war years Paramount developed block booking, a plan whereby exhibitors contracted in advance to buy a number of films to be made within a stipulated time. This plan, helping in great part to effect quantity distribution, was advantageous to producers since it assured them of a steady outlet for their films.

Exhibitors were confronted with the necessity of depending on the block-booking system controlled by the producer-distributors, much to the economic disadvantage of the former. Consequently, this method of sale was opposed almost from its inception by independent exhibitors.

The animosity against block booking became so great that in 1917 27 large exhibitors controlling important theaters in key cities combined and established their own distribution channel—First National Exhibitors Circuit. This organization was established to combat the high prices of big-star pictures and the selling policy of the major producers.[5] Production and distribution units financed by the organization attempted to provide a constant supply of pictures to members. Finally, First National established its own studios.

First National's entry into the production branch had important consequences. The larger producer-distributors lost exhibitor-customers and their market for pictures was threatened. In the case of Famous Players Lasky, stars, directors, and other personnel left for

[5] Principally, Famous Players Lasky Corporation, which through its president, Adolph Zukor, had most of the big name stars under contract and required exhibitors to purchase all their product in order to secure the more popular pictures, like those featuring Mary Pickford.

First National. The trade war extended to problems arising from pricing of pictures, competition for desirable play dates, and the whole problem of booking. In 1918 block booking was temporarily abandoned.

The struggle for supremacy in the industry, formerly based on patent control and market monopoly, now emerged in a fierce battle for theaters. Large theater holdings strengthened bargaining power, and the fight for control of outlets became the order of the day. (See appendix I.) Real estate developments requiring large-scale financial operations led to the almost complete integration of the three branches of the industry—production, distribution, and exhibition—in the hands of the large companies.

By the early twenties, most of the important independent corporations and individuals were eliminated or submerged. The industry had already passed from one of many small independent companies to one controlled by a few relatively powerful organizations.

At this time, a series of Hollywood scandals involving motion picture personalities gave impetus to militant reform groups who were already sponsoring Federal censorship of the movies to reduce the production of salacious pictures. In addition, members of the industry were involved in constant and expensive litigation. The large companies, to provide means for adjusting their internal disputes without recourse to the courts and to combat the censorship movement, in 1922 formed the Motion Picture Producers and Distributors of America, Inc.

The Motion Picture Producers and Distributors of America, Inc., better known as the Hays organization from the political figure employed to be its head, is an illuminating example of the cooperation of large business units for self-protection. It was then, and it is today, supported exclusively by the large companies. It was conceived in fear of regulation of the industry by the public and dedicated to the proposition that outsiders should never dictate its policies.

By 1927, the industry was launched in a period of reckless spending and extravagance which would have meant the inevitable wreck of enterprises in more settled lines. Of necessity, financial dependence on Wall Street increased enormously.

New competition centered on the building of elaborate theaters and bidding in salaries for stars. Admission prices rose to meet increased costs. At the same time, the assembly-line technique was introduced in picture-making. Poor-quality pictures became frequent, and the industry saw a sharp decline in profits.

The sound picture saved the day. Introduced in 1926 by Warner Bros., on the verge of bankruptcy, this innovation received instant approval by the public, and was shortly adopted by the other major companies.

The stock market crash of 1929, coming on the heels of the "talkies" boom, played havoc with some parts of the motion-picture industry as it did with the rest of the Nation. Strangely, though, box-office receipts were not immediately affected.

Wall Street gazed in astonishment at what appeared to be a "depression-proof" industry. The "resistance" of the movie to the stock-market debacle so impressed Wall Street interests that during the following years they were to struggle with more resolution than ever to gain control of the movie industry.[6]

_____
[6] Jacobs, op, cit., p. 300.

The battle for control of sound, started before the crash, now came to its climax. For years, various groups had been experimenting with sound. Warner Bros. developed Vitaphone; Fox developed Movietone. Through alliances with Warner and Fox, Electrical Research Products, Inc. (E. R. P. I.)[7] gained control of their patents. The Radio Corporation of America (R. C. A.)[8] with patent rights to Photophone was E. R. P. I.'s main contender. E. R. P. I. was successful in signing long-term agreements for the use of sound equipment with five of the large producers (M-G-M, Paramount, United Artists, First National, and Universal). These agreements were so successful that R. C. A. was virtually eliminated from the field.[9] Through the Radio-Keith-Orpheum Co. and its large theater holdings, R. C. A. made some headway, but its field was still limited.

R. C. A. finally filed a complaint charging unlawful restraint of trade by American Telephone & Telegraph and its affiliates. In 1935 a peaceful agreement was concluded between the two corporations which gave R. C. A. new and substantial rights.

The entire motion picture industry, therefore, through patent ownership is indirectly under a monopoly control far beyond the early aspirations of the Motion Picture Patents Corporation.[10]

Despite lowered consumer purchasing power due to the depression, sound was at first successful in keeping up the industry's box office receipts. However, the installation of sound equipment in both studios and theaters was a heavy financial burden. As the novelty of sound wore off, box office receipts fell drastically, and the industry finally felt the grip of the depression. The big theater holdings and real estate investments of the motion picture companies swiftly depreciated. Most of the large companies experienced financial difficulties. In 1933 Paramount was adjudicated bankrupt; R-K-O and Universal went into receivership; the Fox Film Corporation was reorganized. Many of the theaters which had been acquired during the earlier program of expansion were dropped. From 1930 to 1935 the number of theaters owned by the major companies declined from 3,600 to 2,225.[11]

One of the consequences of the depression was the enactment in 1933 of the National Industrial Recovery Act. This law required that codes of fair competition, including guarantees of minimum wages, maximum hours, and collective bargaining for labor, and provisions restricting unfair trade practices, be set up for the various industries. The motion picture industry was obliged to adjust itself to the restrictions of a code, but the essential framework of the industry remained unchanged.

The Code of Fair Competition for the Motion Picture Industry, approved November 27, 1933, provided for a Code Authority to administer the code, consisting of five members representing the affiliated interests, five representing unaffiliated interests, three repre-

[7] E. R. P. I. is a subsidiary of Western Electric, which is a subsidiary of American Telephone & Telegraph, Morgan-controlled.

[8] Subsidiary to General Electric, Rockefeller-controlled.

[9] These agreements made it impossible for exhibitors to use R. C. A. sound equipment in theaters with E. R. P. I. equipment. In the fall of 1928, 90 percent of the sound pictures produced were recorded on E. R. P. I. equipment. By the end of 1928 only 95 theaters in the United States contained non-Western Electric reproducing apparatus, while 1,046 theaters had installed Western Electric equipment. (A. R. Danielian, A. T. & T., The Story of Industrial Conquest, Vanguard Press, New York, 1939 pp. 145-149.)

[10] Jacobs, op. cit., p. 421.

[11] "Standard Trade and Securities," published by Standard Statistics Company, "Theaters and Motion Pictures," issue of February 20, 1935, p. TH-47.

sentatives of the Administration without vote, and labor representation when labor problems were to be considered. Despite this appearance of unbiased character, the Code Authority, like the industry, was dominated by the affiliated interests. The Darrow Board report said:

> It was indicated that of the 10 members of the Code Authority, 5 representing affiliated producers, distributors, and exhibitors, and 5 representing unaffiliated producers, distributors, and exhibitors, that only 2 of them were not connected in some way with the affiliated producers, distributors, and exhibitors and could thus·be classed as really independent.[12]

To insure sympathetic administration of the code, the unusual expedient was adopted of naming the members of the Code Authority in the Code itself. In only two other Codes of Fair Competition did this occur.

The same control was seen in the composition of the 31 local grievance boards and 31 local clearance and zoning boards set up under the code to adjudicate motion picture disputes of a local nature.

> They are dominated by the distributors and first-run exhibitors, whose interests are the same. There are only two independent subsequent-run exhibitors provided for on the boards. The interests of distributors and first run theaters being identical as opposed to subsequent-run independent theaters, it is obvious that * * * the voting strength of the boards will be four to two against the independent subsequent-run exhibitors.[13]

Control of the industry remained undisturbed by the code. Nevertheless, independent exhibitors, because of Government intervention, received under the code a number of concessions from the affiliated interests in the way of trade practice reforms. Many of these reforms came to an end after the codes were declared unconstitutional by the Supreme Court on May 27, 1935.

CRYSTALLIZATION OF THE PATTERN

The period of hectic growth and change in the motion-picture industry is over. The early pioneering days have given way to a mature and stabilized business on a grand scale. The bitter competition of yesterday is the close control of today.

All told, there are in the United States about 110 producers, numerous distributors and a multitude of exhibitors. Nevertheless, the industry is dominated by 5 major companies,[14] all of which are active in production, distribution, and exhibition, and 3 satellite companies,[51] interested solely in production and distribution.

The production scene today is one in which about 70 percent of all features produced in this country are made by the 8 major companies. Each of these companies produces from 40 to 60 pictures annually with the exception of United Artists which provides distribution facilities for a group of individual producers who all together make 20 or less.

[12] Report of the National Recovery ·Review (Darrow) Board relating to the Motion Picture Industry, Washington, 1934. Composition of Authority: Representing affiliates, M. H. Aylesworth, president, R. K. O.; S. R. Kent, president, Fox; G. J. Schaefer, vice-president, Paramount; N. M. Schenck, president, Loew's; H. M. Warner, president, Warner's. Representing unaffiliates, R. H. Cochrane, vice president, Universal; W. R. Johnston, president, Republic; E. Kuykendall, president, Motion Picture Theatre Owners of America (including affiliated and unaffiliated theater owners); C. L. O'Reilly, president, Theatre Owners Chamber of Commerce, N. Y.; and N. Yamins, independent exhibitor.
[13] Ibid.
[14] Paramount Pictures, Inc., Loew's, Inc. (Metro-Goldwyn-Mayer), Twentieth Century-Fox Film Corporation, Warner Brothers Pictures, Inc., and Radio-Keith-Orpheum Corporation.
[15] Universal Corporation, Columbia Pictures Corporation, and United Artists Corporation.

TABLE 1.—*Number of feature-length motion pictures produced in the United States by all producing companies, and by each of the major producing companies, by seasons, 1930–31 to 1938–39*

Season [1]	All com-panies	Para-mount	Loew's	Twen-tieth Cen-tury-Fox	Warner	Radio-Keith-Or-pheum	Colum-bia	Univer-sal	United Artists	All other com-panies
1930–31	510	58	43	48	69	32	27	22	13	198
1931–32	490	56	40	46	56	48	31	32	14	167
1932–33	510	51	37	41	53	45	36	28	6	203
1933–34	480	55	44	46	63	40	44	38	20	130
1934–35	520	44	42	40	51	40	39	39	19	206
1935–36	517	50	43	52	58	43	36	27	17	191
1936–37	535	41	40	52	58	39	38	40	19	208
1937–38	450	40	41	49	52	41	39	45	16	127
1938–39	526	58	51	56	54	49	54	45	18	141

[1] Beginning about Sept. 1 each year.

Source: *United States* v. *Paramount Pictures, Inc., et al.*, Civil Action No. 87–273, in the District Court of the United States for the Southern District of New York, amended and supplemental complaint, Nov. 14 1940.

It must be noted that the percentage given above vastly under-states the importance of the major companies in the production branch of the industry. The pictures produced by these companies include practically all of the more pretentious films—those with pro-duction costs of $250,000 or more each. Features produced by inde-pendent companies consist largely of "quickies," westerns and melo-dramas which are not shown in first-class theaters.

The control by the large companies of distribution is even greater. Of the high-quality features which yield the largest box-office returns, during the past five years—

Fox, Loew's, Paramount, R–K–O, and Warner · have * * * collectively released about 80 percent * * * and Columbia, United Artists, and Uni-versal * * * about 15 percent * * *.˙ No other distributor has released more than 1 percent of such features during any of said years and in no year have all other distributors combined released more than 5 percent of such features.[16]

During the same period the first-named 5 majors collectively received about 70 percent and the other 3 about 25 percent of all film rentals in the United States.

Since 1930 the major companies—

have continued to maintain complete control of the distribution of such features, although many of them have been produced by producers not employed by a major company but pursuant to arrangements made preceding the production of such films for release by a major distributor. Such arrangements generally included the use of equipment owned by, or production talent under contract to, one or more of the defendants [majors]. These arrangements have often included financing of the production directly by the major distributor involved or the borrowing of capital by the producer upon its showing that it has been assured of release through a major distributor. Ordinarily, no funds have been or are available for this type of production in the absence of such an assurance.[17]

Independent distributors, therefore, are limited to handling some foreign importations and the "quickie" type of film mentioned above.

Ownership of theaters by producer-distributors has already been indicated as the third link in the pattern of control. Nevertheless, the number of theaters owned today by producer-distributors is not large. Of a total of 17,000 theaters in operation, the majors own or control about 2,800 theaters. About 2,600 of these are individually

[16] *U. S.* v. *Paramount Pictures, Inc., et al.*, Civil Action No. 87–273, in the District Court of the United States for the Southern District of New York, amended and supplemental complaint, Nov. 14, 1940.
[17] Ibid.

owned by the different companies, and about 200 are owned jointly by two of the major companies.[18]

TABLE 2.—*Number of theaters operated by each of the major companies, 1940* [1]

Region and State	Paramount	Loew's	Twentieth Century-Fox	Warner's	Radio-Keith-Orpheum	Total
New England:						
Maine	39					39
New Hampshire	10					10
Vermont	8					8
Massachusetts	82	5		16	5	108
Rhode Island	3	1			2	6
Connecticut	6	10		35		51
Middle Atlantic:						
New York	26	67	1	49	58	201
New Jersey	3	3		92	16	114
Pennsylvania	72	3		195		270
East North Central:						
Ohio	16	10		38	21	85
Indiana	8	3		3		14
Illinois	122		21	19	3	165
Michigan	16		6		7	29
Wisconsin	5		53	19		77
West North Central:						
Minnesota	42				3	45
Iowa	64		6		6	76
Missouri	1	2	48			51
North Dakota	10					10
South Dakota	20					20
Nebraska	14		10		1	25
Kansas			56			56
South Atlantic:						
Delaware		1		6		7
Maryland	1	3		8		12
District of Columbia		4		16	1	21
Virginia	17	2		9		28
West Virginia	3			11	3	17
North Carolina	69			1		70
South Carolina	23					23
Georgia	38	1				39
Florida	109					109
East South Central:						
Kentucky	11	1		8		20
Tennessee	28	2		1		31
Alabama	33					33
Mississippi	35					35
West South Central:						
Arkansas	47					47
Louisiana	20	1			1	22
Oklahoma	6			14		20
Texas	208	1				209
Mountain:						
Montana			17			17
Idaho	9		9			18
Wyoming			14			14
Colorado	9	1	36		1	47
New Mexico	7		6			13
Arizona	8		7			15
Utah	21		2			23
Pacific:						
Washington			28	3		31
Oregon			13	2		15
California	4	1	205	12	4	226
Total	1,273	122	538	557	132	2,622

[1] The table does not include the 200 or more theaters in which some of these companies have a joint interest.

Source *United States* v. *Paramount Pictures, Inc., et al.*, civil action No. 87–273, in the District Court of the United States for the Southern District of New York, amended and supplemental complaint, Nov. 14, 1940

[18] "Each of the producer-exhibitors * * * is jointly interested financially in one or more theaters with one or more of the other producer-exhibitors * * * through profit sharing arrangements with respect to particular theaters; through so-called pools where several theaters owned or controlled by two or more are operated as a unit; through direct or indirect ownership of stock in a single theater operating corporation by two or more of such defendants; or through arrangements where one owns or leases a theater and the other manages it. * * * There are about 200 theaters in the United States in which such joint interests are held, including a substantial number of metropolitan first-run theaters. In addition * * * there are numerous other joint theater interests where executive employees, or managing agents of one producer-exhibitor * * * have direct or indirect stock interests in a theater operating corporation in which another producer-exhibitor * * * also owns a direct or indirect stock interest." (Ibid.)

While these theaters represent but 16 percent of all theaters in operation, they take on added significance when it is noted that more than 80 percent of all metropolitan first-run theaters [19] are affiliated; in 23 key cities all of the first-run theaters are affiliated (table 3); out of 92 cities with population over 100,000 the majors control exhibition in 73 cities (table 4); in these same 73 cities the majors "operate enough first-run theaters in each to receive a substantial majority of the total film revenue supplied by each of these cities"; there are 283 cities with populations between 25,000 and 100,000 in 200 of which the majors operate one or more theaters; "by control of first-run theaters alone, affiliated exhibitors have been able to secure as much as two-thirds of the total theater admissions paid in cities as large as 250,000"; and the affiliates control exhibition in all United States cities with populations of more than 1,000,000.[20]

TABLE 3.—*Number of first-run metropolitan theaters operated by each of the major companies in 35 key cities, 1940*

City	Paramount	Loew's	Twentieth Century-Fox	Warner Bros.	Radio-Keith-Orpheum
Albany, N. Y.[1]				2	2
Atlanta, Ga	4	1			
Baltimore, Md		1		1	
Boston, Mass.[1]	4	2			
Brooklyn, N. Y.[1]	1	1		1	2
Charlotte, N. C.[1]	3			1	
Chicago, Ill.[1]	6				1
Cincinnati, Ohio[1]					6
Cleveland, Ohio[1]		2		2	2
Dallas, Tex.[1]	6				
Denver, Colo.		1	4		1
Des Moines, Iowa[1]	4				1
Detroit, Mich.	5			1	
Houston, Tex.[1]	3	1			
Indianapolis, Ind.		1			
Kansas City, Mo.[1]		1	3		
Los Angeles, Calif.			5	2	2
Memphis, Tenn.[1]	2	1		1	
Milwaukee, Wis.[1]			3	1	
Minneapolis, Minn.[1]	6				1
Newark, N. J.[1]	1	1		2	2
New Haven, Conn.[1]	1	2		1	
New Orleans, La.[1]	3	1			1
New York City	1	2	1	2	1
Oklahoma City, Okla.[1]				7	
Omaha, Nebr.[1]	3				1
Philadelphia, Pa.[1]				8	
Pittsburgh, Pa.		1		2	
Portland, Oreg.			4		
Salt Lake City, Utah[1]	6				
St. Louis, Mo.		1			
St. Paul, Minn.[1]	4				2
San Francisco, Calif.		1	4		1
Seattle, Wash.			5		
Washington, D. C.[1]		3		2	1
Total	63	24	30	35	29

[1] In cities thus marked, all first-run theaters are operated by these companies.

Source: *United States* v. *Paramount Pictures, Inc., et al.*, civil action No. 87–273, in the District Court of the United States for the Southern District of New York, amended and supplemental complaint, Nov. 14, 1940.

[19] A metropolitan theater is one located in a key city. A key city is one of such size and strategic location that the first-run exhibition of a motion picture therein effectively advertises the film among exhibitors and the public in a wide surrounding area; 31 such cities constitute the main distributing centers of the major companies. A first-run theater is one which exhibits first-class features released by one or more of the majors on a first-run showing in the city or town in which it is located. An affiliated theater is one which is either owned or controlled by 1 of the 5 major producer-distributor-exhibitor companies.
[20] *United States* v. *Paramount*, 1940.

TABLE 4.—*Cities with populations of 100,000 or more in which exhibition is controlled by major companies*

City	Population rank [1]	Controlled by—
New York, N. Y	1	Loew's, Paramount, R-K-O, Warner.
Chicago, Ill	2	Paramount, R-K-O, Warner.
Philadelphia, Pa	3	Fox, Paramount, Warner.
Detroit, Mich	4	Fox, Paramount.
Los Angeles, Calif	5	Fox, Loew's, Paramount, R-K-O, Warner.
Cleveland, Ohio	6	Loew's, R-K-O, Warner.
Boston, Mass	9	Loew's, Paramount, R-K-O.
Pittsburgh, Pa	10	Loew's, Warner.
Washington, D. C	11	Loew's, R-K-O, Warner.
San Francisco, Calif	12	Fox, Loew's, Paramount, R-K-O.
Milwaukee, Wis	13	Fox, Warner.
Buffalo, N. Y	14	Loew's, Paramount.
New Orleans, La	15	Loew's, Paramount, R-K-O.
Minneapolis, Minn	16	Paramount, R-K-O.
Cincinnati, Ohio	17	R-K-O.
Newark, N. J	18	Loew's, Paramount, R-K-O, Warner.
Kansas City, Mo	19	Fox, Loew's, Paramount.
Houston, Tex	21	Loew's, Paramount.
Seattle, Wash	22	Fox.
Rochester, N. Y	23	Loew's, Paramount, R-K-O.
Denver, Colo	25	Fox, Loew's, R-K-O.
Portland, Oreg	26	Fox.
Columbus, Ohio	27	Loew's, R-K-O.
Oakland, Calif	28	Fox.
Atlanta, Ga	29	Loew's, Paramount.
Jersey City, N. J	30	Loew's, R-K-O, Warner.
Dallas, Tex	31	Paramount.
Memphis, Tenn	32	Loew's, Paramount, Warner.
St. Paul, Minn	33	Paramount, R-K-O.
Birmingham, Ala	35	Paramount.
San Antonio, Tex	37	Paramount, Warner.
Omaha, Nebr	39	Paramount, R-K-O.
Dayton, Ohio	40	Loew's, R-K-O.
Syracuse, N. Y	41	Loew's, R-K-O, Warner.
Oklahoma City, Okla	42	Paramount, Warner.
San Diego, Calif	43	Fox.
Worcester, Mass	44	Loew's, Paramount, Warner.
Richmond, Va	45	Loew's.
Fort Worth, Tex	46	Paramount.
Jacksonville, Fla	47	Do.
Miami, Fla	48	Do.
Youngstown, Ohio	49	Warner.
Hartford, Conn	51	Loew's, Paramount, Warner.
Grand Rapids, Mich	52	Paramount, R-K-O.
Long Beach, Calif	53	Fox.
New Haven, Conn	54	Loew's, Paramount, Warner.
Des Moines, Iowa	55	Paramount, R-K-O.
Flint, Mich	56	Do.
Salt Lake City, Utah	57	Paramount.
Springfield, Mass	58	Loew's, Paramount, Warner.
Bridgeport, Conn	59	Loew's, Warner.
Norfolk, Va	60	Loew's.
Yonkers, N. Y	61	Loew's, Paramount, R-K-O.
Scranton, Pa	63	Paramount.
Paterson, N. J	64	Paramount, Warner.
Albany, N. Y	65	R-K-O, Warner.
Chattanooga, Tenn	66	Paramount.
Trenton, N. J	67	R-K-O.
Spokane, Wash	68	Fox.
Camden, N. J	71	Warner.
Erie, Pa	72	Do.
Wichita, Kans	74	Fox.
Knoxville, Tenn	75	Paramount.
Wilmington, Del	76	Loew's, Warner.
Reading, Pa	79	Do.
Tampa, Fla	83	Paramount.
Sacramento, Calif	85	Fox.
Peoria, Ill	86	Paramount.
South Bend, Ind	88	Do.
Lowell, Mass	89	Paramount, R-K-O.
Utica, N. Y	90	Warner.
Charlotte, N. C	91	Paramount.
Duluth, Minn	92	Do.

[1] All population figures are taken from 1940 census.

Source: *United States* v. *Paramount Pictures, Inc., et al.*, civil action No. 87–273, in the District Court of the United States for the Southern District of New York, amended and supplemental complaint, Nov. 14, 1940.

More important than the percentage of theaters owned is the seating capacity represented therein, estimated at about 25 percent of the total seating capacity in the United States. This situation is illustrated by a tabulation of theaters and seating capacity in three large cities—Philadelphia, Chicago, and Milwaukee—and the State of Florida. Moreover, these seats in larger and better houses represent an even larger proportion of potential box-office returns, since admission prices in these more important theaters are usually considerably higher than in other theaters, and they operate a greater number of hours per week than the smaller houses.

TABLE 5.—*Control of exhibition facilities by a single major company in each of 4 localities, 1939*

	Theaters [1]		Seats		Average number of seats per theater
	Number	Percent of total	Number	Percent of total	
Philadelphia, Pa.	203	100.0	203,616	100.0	1,003
Warner Bros. Circuit Management Corporation	58	28.6	85,019	41.8	1,466
Chicago, Ill.	309	100.0	328,379	100.0	1,063
Balaban & Katz Corporation [2]	38	12.3	84,919	25.9	2,235
Milwaukee, Wis.	66	100.0	72,186	100.0	1,094
Fox Wisconsin circuit	15	22.7	18,550	25.7	1,237
State of Florida	214	100.0	122,172	100.0	571
Paramount Pictures, Inc. [3]	· 68	31.8	54,534	44.6	802

[1] Those theaters are excluded which were closed or for which seating capacity was not given.
[2] Balaban & Katz Corporation is 97 percent controlled by Paramount Pictures, Inc.
[3] Includes only theaters operated by E. J. Sparks and S. A. Lynch. Paramount operates approximately 40 additional theaters in Florida.

Source: Compiled from data in the 1940 Film Daily Yearbook.

Thus integration in the motion picture industry is complete, from the inception of an idea for a picture through to the actual exhibition of the film. The importance of the integration of production, distribution, and exhibition lies in the accomplishment, not of more closely knit operation but of virtual elimination of competition.

In the production field, competition between the major companies has been minimized since 1930 by the device of loaning talent.

The major producers have preferred to loan and exchange the highest priced technical and artistic talent which they may have under exclusive contract to and with each other on standardized terms rather than drive the price of such talent higher by competing for the privilege of placing it under contract in the first instance.[21]

These same privileges have not been accorded independent producers.

Even where such talent has been made available to independent producers, the terms have frequently been discriminatory as compared to the terms upon which it has been made available to major producers.[22]

[21] Ibid.
[22] Ibid.

TABLE 6.—*Number of loans by major companies since 1933* [1]

Major company	To major producers	To independent producers	Major company	To major producers	To independent producers
Loew's	610	56	Fox	251	7
Paramount	439	46	Columbia	175	36
Warner	223	12	Universal	198	11
R-K-O	109	12			

[1] Loans of stars, feature players, directors, writers, cameramen, or other production talent under contract to one major producer made to another producer.

Source: *U. S.* v. *Paramount Pictures, Inc., et al.*, civil action No. 87-273, in the District Court of the United States for the Southern District of New York, amended and supplemental complaint, Nov. 14, 1940.

Cooperation between the big producers is not limited to exchange of talent. Through the Association of Motion Picture Producers, Inc. (see appendix 2), which operates the Call Bureau and Central Casting Corporation, the majors in effect have established a common personnel department to provide themselves with extra and bit players below the contract grade. These services are not extended to non-members.

Production of pictures by independents is impeded by lack of good distribution facilities. To obtain loans from banks in order to start production, the independents must be assured good distribution.

If the producer has a good distributing contract * * * and that picture is distributed through a reputable distributing company that knows how to sell the picture, I might loan as high as the entire cost of production. I do not do that always, but if there is a good distributing contract in a good distributing organization * * * I will not hesitate to loan the entire cost of production.[23]

A pretentious film, in order to be profitable, must be shown in at least some of the better-class theaters controlled by the major companies. The only way an independent producer can insure this is through a distribution contract with one of the major companies.

It is difficult to believe that capital will readily enter a field of business where conditional requirements exist, if aware in advance of restrictions which either partially or entirely close the market to the products of the projected undertaking.[24]

Independent production and distribution of a first-class feature is thus indeed rare. In fact, "more than 95 percent of the features exhibited in metropolitan first-run theaters are released by" the major companies.[25]

In the beginning, when the major companies were acquiring theaters at a rapid pace, these companies frequently found themselves in competition in the exhibition field. Here, as elsewhere, it was decided that cooperation is more profitable than competition. Each company acquired and relinquished interests in theaters, but in time there was a tendency for one company to emerge as the dominant element in a particular geographical area.

The affiliated companies have each retained well-scattered interests in large prior-run theaters in metropolitan locations, but have tended less and less to compete in the operation of the smaller or subsequent-run theaters. In some cases affiliated companies have withdrawn in favor of the dominant element. In other cases conflicting interests

[23] "Story of the Films," edited by Joseph P. Kennedy, A. W. Shaw Co., Chicago and New York, 1927, p. 87. Discussion by Dr. Attilio H. Giannini, then president, Bowery & East River National Bank, formerly president of United Artists.
[24] W. H. S. Stevens, "Unfair Competition," University of Chicago Press, 1917, p. 76.
[25] *United States* v. *Paramount Pictures, Inc.*, 1940.

have been resolved by joint operation agreements whereby one company assumes the responsibility of operation but both share in the profits. Gradually, the major companies have acquired rather separate and distinct areas or spheres of control.

Paramount, operating more than 1,200 theaters, has the largest exhibition holdings among the major companies. About half of Paramount's theaters are located in the South. In that broad area comprising the States of North Carolina, South Carolina, Georgia, Florida, Tennessee, Alabama, Mississippi, Arkansas, Louisiana, and Texas the other major companies operate but a handful of theaters, and virtually every one of these is a large first-run theater in a key city. A similar pattern is found in North Dakota, South Dakota, Minnesota, Iowa, eastern Nebraska, northern Illinois, and Utah. Paramount is the sole affiliated exhibitor in the New England States of Maine, New Hampshire, and Vermont, and it operates an important number of theaters in Massachusetts. Important groups of Paramount theaters are also found in Pennsylvania, Virginia, Indiana, Ohio, and Colorado.

Fox has well over 500 theaters. These are primarily located in the Pacific and Mountain States of California, Oregon, Washington, Montana, Wyoming, and Colorado, and in this area there are relatively few other affiliated theaters. Also, in the Middle West, Fox is the sole affiliated exhibitor in Kansas and western Nebraska and has the major share in Missouri and Wisconsin.

Warner's operates more than 500 theaters. These are located principally in the Atlantic Coast States with the largest holdings in Pennsylvania, New Jersey, New York, and Connecticut. It has an appreciable number of theaters in Massachusetts, the District of Columbia, Maryland, Delaware, and the Virginias. Warner's also has important exhibition interests in Ohio, Illinois, Wisconsin, Oklahoma, and Kentucky.

R-K-O has over 100 theaters, more than half of which are in New York and New Jersey. It has an appreciable number in Ohio and Michigan and about 30 in 10 other States.

Loew's operates the smallest number of theaters of any of the majors—120–130. More than half of these theaters are in New York City. There is also an appreciable number of Loew theaters in Connecticut and Ohio. The remainder are scattered throughout the country and are among the best first-run theaters in large cities.[26]

A description of the theater holdings of the major companies in such broad terms does not indicate clearly just how neatly the exhibition interests of these companies are segregated. This is best seen when the theater holdings of the major companies are mapped according to their exact locations. If this be done, it is seen that although both Paramount and Warner's have important exhibition interests in the State of Pennsylvania, the theaters of each company are so located as not to compete with one another. Warner's theaters are located in the western part of the State around Pittsburgh and in the southeastern corner centering in Philadelphia. Most of the Paramount theaters, on the other hand, are in the northeast section of the State, in the Scranton and Wilkes-Barre area, with a few theaters clustered together on the extreme west border of the State.

---

[26] Loew's has always pursued a very conservative policy regarding theater acquisitions. "Outside of New York, home of the big Loew neighborhood chain, there are only five Loew theaters that are not first-run." (Fortune, vol. XX, No. 2, August 1939.)

Warner's theater holdings in the neighborhood of Philadelphia extend into the northern tip of Delaware and across the Susquehanna River into Camden and southern New Jersey.   Warner's also operates a number of theaters in northern New Jersey.   The center of the State, however, is dominated by R-K-O which has about 15 theaters in the neighborhood of Trenton.

Loew's and R-K-O both have important chains of neighborhood theaters in New York City.   Neither of these companies, however, has extended its holdings into the New York counties immediately to the North.   These are dominated by Paramount.   Further upstate the picture again changes, and there are groups of R-K-O and Warner theaters.   Paramount theaters again appear in pooled operation with Loew in Buffalo and with R-K-O in Rochester.

Nor does the above indicate the number of situations in which two of the major companies jointly operate theaters.   In addition to the more than 2,600 theaters which are individually operated by one of the majors, there are, as previously mentioned, more than 200 others operated jointly through pooling agreements.   Each one of the major companies has a joint operation agreement for at least one theater with at least one of the other affiliated companies.   A most important instance of such operation is in Michigan.   In the peninsula area, outside the city of Detroit, Paramount and R-K-O are jointly interested in the operation of over 100 theaters.   These theaters represent practically the entire affiliated theater interests in this area.[27]

This division of the exhibition branch of the industry into separate areas of control has not only eliminated competition in exhibition between the major companies, but also has made each major company the dominant element in every territory in which it operates, even where opposed by powerful independent interests.   Acting as an exhibitor, each of the companies is able to count upon the goodwill of the other companies in meeting independent competition since it is expected that preferential treatment will be reciprocated in areas where these other companies act as exhibitors.

The granting of certain terms and privileges with respect to the exhibition of one producer-exhibitor's * * * films in another producer-exhibitor's * * * circuit is necessarily conditioned upon the granting of similar terms and privileges by the latter with respect to the exhibition of its films in the circuit of the former.[28]

Competition in the motion picture industry today is far different than when the industry was composed of a great many small units.   At the present time there is competition between the large producer-distributor-exhibitor units, but it is limited.   The problem of securing name actors, actresses, and directors is to some extent solved by mutual loaning of personnel.   The producers have eliminated the problem of marketing motion pictures by taking over into their own control the most important theaters in the country—those from which the major share of revenue comes.   In general, competition between the exhibition units of the large companies has been avoided by a division of the exhibition field into separate spheres of influence.

In lieu of competition between the leaders of the industry, there is in many respects a very definite cooperation.   This is illustrated by

---

[27] Ibid. and The Film Daily Yearbook, 1940.
[28] United States v. Paramount, 1940.

the Hays organization, the avowed purpose of which is self-government of the industry.   Through the many divisions and services of this organization, the major producer-distributor-exhibitors engage in many common activities, and present a united front against any influence which would tend to change the status quo.   (See appendix II.)

The state of competition in the industry is epitomized in the utterance of Spyros Skouras, executive of one of the affiliated exhibition companies and himself owner of a large theater chain.   After urging an increase of admission prices to a minimum of 50 cents in all principal key cities, he added:

For we are no longer fighting each other, nor is there any longer such a thing as competition, but a question of establishing solidarity or perishing.[29]

[29] Film Daily, June 7, 1940.

CHAPTER II

THE ISSUES

CHAPTER II

THE ISSUES

When a few dominating elements finally achieve substantial control of an industry, they usually proceed to adopt and perfect methods which will insure retention of that control. Such methods commonly lead to protests of unfair advantage, not only from smaller elements within the industry, but in some cases from consumers as well. It is not surprising that, as in most instances where conflicts of interest arise, a slogan summarizing the grievances of these parties usually appears. In industrial warfare, the rallying cry frequently becomes the name of some trade practice.

Every industry, as a normal consequence to the conditions under which it operates, develops its own peculiar trade practices. However, frequent attacks on a practice do not constitute proof that it is in itself vicious. Instead, the difficulty usually lies in the way the trade practice is employed. A practice, which under other circumstances might be wholly innocent, may provide a perfect instrument of control when used as a tool in the hands of a dominating element within an industry.

The motion picture industry has perhaps developed more than its share of odd trade practices. Many of these arise from the unusual circumstance that the industry operates basically under the copyright laws rather than the laws of purchase and sale. In most industries the manufacturer (producer) sells his product to a wholesaler (distributor) who in turn sells it to a retailer (exhibitor), and the retailer finally places the product in the hands of the consumer. Title to the product in such circumstances has thus changed hands several times during the transit of the goods from the manufacturer to the consumer.

In the motion picture industry, on the other hand, the producer makes a negative film from which are reproduced a number of positive prints. The film is protected by copyright, and both this copyright and title to the actual films seldom change hands. Since the producer and distributor are usually a part of the same company, it is immaterial which holds the actual title. The film is rented to the exhibitor who is simultaneously licensed under the copyright privilege to exhibit the film to the public. No physical exchange of goods for money takes place between the exhibitor and the consumer. The film is shown, and the print is returned to the distributor who ships it on to another exhibitor. Each film is thus used many times, crossing and recrossing State lines as it is leased and shipped to one exhibitor after another.

Since actual title is never acquired by the exhibitor, the distributor is able under the copyright laws to exercise control over the use of the print by the exhibitor. He is able to determine at what time and to a large extent under what conditions the exhibitor shall show the pictures to his audiences. This contrasts with the retailer in most lines of enterprise who is generally less restricted in the disposition of his product.

Another unusual circumstance in the motion picture industry is the perishableness of the product handled. The necessity or desirability of showing a picture to the public while it is still new makes freshness or priority in vending the product to the public a most important factor.

Thus, it is found that most of the unusual trade practices of the industry, and coincidentally most of its controversies, arise either from the special legal privileges accorded a copyright holder or from the efforts to show the product while it is still new.

The principal objective of the industry is, of course, to show films to the consumer, and this takes place through the medium of the exhibitor. Naturally, therefore, it is the exhibitor—the link between the producer-distributor and the consumer—who is involved in most of the controversies of the industry.

Each exhibitor has two important relationships with other elements in the industry. One concerns his contact with the distributors from whom he must secure supplies of film. The other affects the exhibitors with whom he is in competition for a supply of film and for priority of showing.

Looking first at the distributors, we find that virtually all first-quality feature films produced in the United States are distributed through eight companies. Thus, where the supply of films is concerned, the exhibitor faces a high degree of concentration.

With respect to relations between exhibitors, it is found that most theaters are operated singly or in groups of two or three. In other cases, however, a great many theaters may be tied together under common management and control to form a single large chain exhibition organization. The number of theaters acting together as a single bargaining unit in this way may run into the hundreds. The small exhibitor is thus frequently in competition with a large and financially powerful organization, which perhaps is still further reinforced by affiliation with one of the major producer-distributors.

Claims of unfair business tactics are most usually advanced by the smaller elements within an industry. The very size of the larger units gives them power, and this power is their protection. The controversies usually involve claims by the smaller elements that the larger organizations misuse the power granted them by their size to stifle or eliminate competition.

Accordingly, most of the controversies of the motion picture industry may be divided into two general classes. One class includes those practices which, according to small exhibitors, are used by the large distributor organizations to maximize their profits at the expense of the exhibitors and the public. In this category may be placed block booking, blind selling, forcing of short subjects, and designating of play dates. The other class comprises those practices which small exhibitors contend have been used by large exhibitor organizations to drive them out of business or place them in subordinate competitive positions. Under this heading are such practices as overbuying, setting of admission prices, and clearance and zoning.

Of course, not all aspects of these practices may be so neatly divided into two such general classes. Since the five largest companies in the industry act not only as the most important producers and distributors of motion pictures but also as the operators of a large number of the best and most profitable theaters in the United States, these categories to some extent merge. Nevertheless, the distinction is useful in analyzing the problems and controversies of the industry.

BLOCK BOOKING, BLIND SELLING, AND THE FORCING OF SHORT SUBJECTS

Block booking.—This practice has been defined as the simultaneous sale by a distributor to an exhibitor of a number of motion pictures for release and delivery over a period of time. The pictures are offered in a group, and the aggregate price is in part determined by the quantity taken.

A distinction is sometimes made between block booking as such and compulsory block booking. In the latter case, an exhibitor is offered the entire group of films handled by a distributor during a single season. He is required to purchase the entire block under some designated terms or is given to understand that he will be unable to license any. In some cases, while the pictures may not be offered on an "all or none" basis, the price of pictures selected individually may be placed so high as to make purchase of anything less than the entire block not feasible.

Perhaps more than any other trade practice of the motion picture industry, block booking has been brought before the public and debated as an evil or a blessing. It has been attacked by independent exhibitors, by independent producers, by the Federal Trade Commission, and by consumer groups. It has been discussed in legislatures and reviewed in the courts.

The most persistent attacks on block booking have come from independent exhibitors. In the first place, each of the major producer-distributors (excepting United Artists, which distributes a smaller number of high-quality films) makes and attempts to sell from 40 to 60 or more feature pictures each year. The exhibitor, depending on his policy with respect to changes of program and double features, may use during a single year as many as several hundred features.

Ideally, the exhibitor would prefer to select from the offerings of each distributor those pictures he considers most in keeping with his exhibition requirements. Where compulsory block booking is exercised, however, this is not possible. The exhibitor finds it necessary to contract for the entire output of several distributors, regardless of the quality or desirability of the individual pictures making up each block. In this way, independent exhibitors are effectively prevented from developing individuality for their theaters, based on their personal tastes and knowledge of their audiences.

Further, because of the necessity of contracting for films in large blocks, exhibitors on some occasions are compelled to contract for more pictures than they can profitably show. It is important to note that once a contract has been executed, it is economically necessary for the exhibitor to show the films, since whether they are shown or not, he must pay for them.

Contracts between distributors and exhibitors usually contain the following stipulation under the heading "Liquidated Damages":

If the Exhibitor shall fail or refuse to exhibit during the term hereof, any of said motion pictures, the Exhibitor shall pay as liquidated damages a sum equal to the fixed sum or sums herein specified as the rental for each such motion picture * * *.[1]

In addition, the complete preemption of playing time after a few block purchases have been made limits the ability of the exhibitor to contract for desirable films of other producers should they be made available to him. It is important to point out that exhibitors do not object to block booking as such, since assurance of a continuous supply of film is an important consideration. Rather, it is the compulsory nature of the practice which they oppose.

The independent exhibitors have been supported in their opposition by religious, civic, and public welfare groups. These groups oppose block booking because it interferes with community selection, or local censorship activities. It is the experience of these groups that an exhibitor will meet their objections to the showing of an unsuitable film with the statement that he is economically obliged to play it since he must pay for it, or alternatively that failure to show it might involve him in a breach of contract action.

The practice is attacked by independent producers who, in trying to sell their product to independent exhibitors, find playing time preempted by block purchases, leaving little or no screen time for their product. This same reason tends to discourage the entry of new producers into the industry.[2]

On the other side, block booking has been defended by the affiliated producer-distributors as a method of wholesaling which reduces their distribution costs. Further, they allege that the definite income assured them by the practice enables them to make better pictures than they could otherwise.

The present interest is not in the claims of these conflicting industry groups; rather it is in determining whether the practice adversely or beneficially affects the public.

The consumer usually patronizes the theater convenient to him. Geographically, therefore, he is limited in his choice of pictures. If the theater is under block-booking contracts which prevent the proprietor from selecting pictures he feels are suitable for his audience or which require him to show inferior pictures, the interests of the consumer are not served.

The system assures an income on many pictures which can by no standard be called excellent. The economic reason for the curtailment of low-quality productions is thus weakened. It may be assumed that a system of free licensing would give additional impetus to the production of higher-quality pictures.

It is alleged that block booking is used as one of the devices of control whereby competition between producers in the licensing of pictures is to some extent lessened. Such competition as exists at present is, for the most part, confined to a brief selling season in the late summer or early fall of each year. Year-round competitive sales efforts and the fluctuating market prices that are thus implied are not found in this industry. Moreover the sale of pictures in large blocks obviates a good deal of the price competition between pictures which might take place were each film's probable box-office attractiveness to be weighed against its asking price. It may be assumed that under a

[1] Hearings before the Committee on Interstate and Foreign Commerce, House of Representatives, pursuant to S. 280, 76th Congress, third session, "Motion-Picture Films," Part I, Paramount Exhibition Contract, p. 230.
[2] Ibid. See testimony of I. E. Chadwick, pp. 344–368.

system where each picture would have to stand on its individual merits, there would be greater price competition in film rentals.

The preemption of industry playing time by large block purchases to a large extent limits the market for new independent producers. However, it must be pointed out that the control of the more important exhibition outlets by the producer-distributors is probably a more important factor in limiting the entrance of new producers of quality pictures into the market than is block booking.

If the producer contention that block booking is an economical method of distribution which reduces distribution costs is valid, this is to the advantage of the consumer. It is unquestionably true that sale of pictures in smaller groups than the total offered by a distributor during a single season would entail greater sales expense. However, distribution costs in toto are relatively small, and sales expense is but a fraction of distribution cost.[3] The savings in sales expense achieved by block booking may thus represent a doubtful economy for the consumer if the system entails even minor disadvantages of other types.

Likewise, it is advantageous to the consumer, if, as producers contend, assured income permits the production of better pictures. It might be argued that conspicuous success in this direction has not yet been achieved, although block booking has been in effect for more than 20 years. Moreover, the large box-office returns from some pictures produced on small budgets, compared with occasional expensive box-office failures, indicates that success in satisfying the consumer is not wholly to be measured in terms of income available for production.[4] To the contrary, there is strong reason to believe that a more competitive system of sales would tend to discourage the production of poor pictures, in contrast to the present system which insures a return on even the least satisfactory films of the major producers.

A weighing of these pros and cons leads to the conclusion that block booking as practiced today is, on the whole, disadvantageous to the consumer. It is necessary, however, to examine the alternatives.

The most frequent proposal has been that compulsory block booking be completely eliminated. In practically every Congress in the last 15 years bills to that effect have been introduced,[5] but none has passed both Houses. The latest of these was the Neely bill, which states in section 3:

It shall be unlawful for any distributor of motion-picture films in commerce to lease or offer to lease for public exhibition films in a block or group of two or more films at a designated lump-sum price for the entire block or group only and to require the exhibitor to lease all such films or permit him to lease none; or to lease or offer to lease for public exhibition films in a block or group of two or more at a designated lump-sum price for the entire block or group and at separate and several prices for separate and several films, or for a number or numbers thereof less than the total number, which total or lump-sum price and separate and several prices shall bear to each such relation (a) as to operate as an unreasonable

[3] According to the industry, distribution costs amount to 10 percent of the motion-picture dollar. ("Film Facts," published by the Motion Picture Producers and Distributors of America, Inc., New York, 1940.) Recent data are not available, but in 1929 motion picture distributors affiliated with producers reported total expenses of $31,700,000. Of this amount $9,700,000 was accounted for by salaries and expenses of salesmen. (U. S. Dept. of Commerce, Census of Distribution, 1929.) In this year, then, direct sales expense amounted to less than one-third of total distribution expenses. There is no reason to assume that the proportion has materially altered since that time.
[4] For example, "The Great McGinty" and "It Happened One Night," produced on relatively small budgets, were financial successes, while "Marco Polo," produced on a lavish scale, was a failure.
[5] Among them are: S. 1667, 70th Cong., 1st sess.; S. 3012, H. R. 4757, H. R. 8877, and H. R. 6472, 74th Cong., 2d sess.; S. 280, 76th Cong., 3d sess.

restraint upon the freedom of an exhibitor to select and lease for use and exhibition only such film or films of such block or group as he may desire and prefer to procure for exhibition, or (b) as tends to require an exhibitor to lease such entire block or group or forego the lease of any number or numbers thereof, or (c) that the effect of the lease or offer to lease of such films may be substantially to lessen competition or tend to create a monopoly in the production, distribution, and exhibition of films; or to lease or offer to lease for public exhibition films in any other manner or by any other means the effect of which would be to defeat the purpose of this Act.[6]

The major difficulty which such a provision would face in practice is that the magnitude of the price differential which would constitute an unreasonable restraint upon an exhibitor's choice of pictures or which would substantially lessen competition is not explicitly defined. The interpretation of the provision would thus be left to the courts. A variety of judgments not necessarily in consonance with each other might well arise, and there is little doubt that both the industry and the already crowded courts would be plunged into a new period of extensive and costly litigation.

The Federal Trade Commission in 1927 attempted to outlaw the practice by issuing a "cease and desist" order against Famous Players-Lasky Corporation [7] in which it declared that block booking was an unfair and improper practice. The ruling was later reversed by the Federal courts.[8] Trade practice hearings conducted by the Federal Trade Commission in 1927 resulted in little change as the Commission was unable to secure agreement between all factions in the industry.

Another alternative to block booking which has been proposed is the cancelation privilege. It has been suggested that many of the disadvantages of block booking would be eliminated if the exhibitor were given the privilege of canceling a stated proportion of all films bought in groups without having to make payment therefor. One of the early proposals of this type was the "5–5–5" clause, so called because under it exhibitors were permitted to cancel 5 percent without payment, 5 percent with half payment, and 5 percent with full payment (but with extended playing time on other features) of all pictures bought in block, provided the block included all features released by the distributor during a season. This clause was drawn up as a result of meetings between distributors and exhibitors during 1928 and 1930; it was not, however, extensively adopted. It was superseded in 1933 by a 10 percent cancelation clause incorporated in the Code for the Motion Picture Industry set up under the National Recovery Administration.[9]

Under the Code provisions, exhibitors were given the privilege of canceling without payment up to 10 percent of all films bought in blocks. Exercise of the cancelation privilege was, however, hemmed about with many restrictions which, according to exhibitor testimony before the Darrow Board and House and Senate hearings, made the privilege of little value to them.[10] Some form of cancelation clause has remained in the licensing agreements of many of the companies since the N. R. A. codes were invalidated. The following illustrates the type of provision usually found at the present time.

* * * If the total number of feature motion pictures offered to the Exhibitor by the Distributor, at one time, shall have been licensed by the Distributor here-

[6] S. 280, 77th Cong., 1st sess.
[7] Federal Trade Commission, Docket No. 835, July 9, 1927.
[8] *Federal Trade Commission* v. *Paramount Famous-Lasky. Corporation*, Adolph Zukor, and Jesse L. Lasky, in the United States Circuit Court of Appeals for the Second Circuit, April 4, 1932.
[9] National Recovery Administration, Code of Fair Competition for the Motion Picture Industry, article V–F, Part 6, of the approved Code, 1933.
[10] See National Recovery Administration, Work Materials, No. 34, 1936, pp. 93–96.

under, the Exhibitor shall have the right to exclude from this license not to exceed ten (10%) percent of the total number of feature motion pictures so licensed hereunder provided the Exhibitor shall give to the Distributor written notice of the Exhibitor's election to exclude any of said motion pictures within ten (10) days after the mailing by the Distributor of notice of availability thereof. Upon the exclusion of each feature motion picture the license therefor and all rights thereunder shall terminate and shall revert to the Distributor.[11]

The intent of such a clause is that exhibitors have the right to a 10-percent cancelation of undesirable pictures if certain conditions are adhered to: They must contract for the whole block offered; they must not be in default of their contract (any default making them liable for the amount involved in those pictures already canceled); they must give the distributor notice of cancelation in the time specified; they must have paid for nine pictures before canceling one (the cancelation privilege being cumulative).

There is reason to believe that insertion by distributors of a cancelation clause in film contracts has been largely a political gesture. The clause has permitted producer-distributors to contend at the repeated Congressional hearings on block booking that they have taken steps to correct any abuses with which the practice might be charged—that they have, in fact, been more liberal in their treatment of exhibitors under block contracts than strictly necessary.

It may be noted, in the first place, that cancelation does not cost the industry any playing time. The screen time allotted a canceled picture must be filled by some other attraction. But beyond this, exhibitors have repeatedly alleged at House and Senate hearings on block booking that such cancelation privileges as have been voluntarily extended to them by distributors have by various means been rendered wholly ineffective.

One method of circumvention considered particularly obnoxious has been that of reallocation. Pictures are customarily classified according to quality, and become known as "A" pictures, "B" pictures, and so on. The classification is subject to the control of the distributor, and the rental asked for a film is made according to the class allocation. At the time he executes a block contract, an exhibitor may know only that he has contracted for a specified number of A, B, and C pictures. After he makes known his intention to cancel a particular film, he may find that it is reallocated to the lowest price group while some other film in a lower class has increased in price.

In one case cited, an exhibitor canceled a picture in the A class because the women in his community did not want it shown. This picture, originally allocated at $138, was reallocated at $23 in the lowest bracket. Another picture, eighteenth in quality and showing bad box office returns was then reallocated to this exhibitor at $138 in place of the cancelation.[12]

An exhibitor, after canceling a poor picture, may be told that the print of a desirable attraction is unavailable; it may be intimated that the print will later become available if the cancelation is withdrawn.

To avoid promiscuous use of the cancelation privilege and to hurry the playing of undesirable films, use has been made of the "stop" picture. The "stop" picture is any attraction which has been shown successfully in the first-run houses and is much in demand among theatergoers. It is employed by distributors primarily to force

---

[11] Hearings, House of Representatives, pursuant to S. 280, p. 433.
[12] Ibid, p. 428, also contracts showing reallocation on pp. 439–440.

exhibitors to "fulfill their contractual obligations" (that is, to send immediately a check for any film rentals which may be due), but it is also used to induce exhibitors to play undesired films.

I screened The Tower of London and because of the horror it contained, I deemed the picture unfit to show at the Lyric Theater * * * I, thereupon, called the Universal manager * * * and attempted to cancel it out. He assured me I would make a lot of money and I had better play the picture. I, however, still did not wish to play it and so I wrote him * * * attempting to cancel.

That letter * * * will give you a summary and story of his reaction to my attempts to cancel. Finally, I had to pay for the picture in order to get Destry Rides Again, and not play it. I did this and still have not played the picture, nor do I intend to play it.[13]

It has also been alleged that distributors can easily circumvent a cancelation privilege by including with releases a few definitely unsatisfactory and cheap pictures, knowing that the privilege will be used up on these films.

The significance of the cancelation privilege as a remedy to block booking is succinctly stated by Nathan Yamins, a leading independent exhibitor.

* * * the cancelation privilege offers no remedy to the evils of block booking. These provisions still enable the producer-distributor to maintain their monopoly on the screen, it still enables the distributor to pass on his mistakes to the exhibitor, and with the exception of the top group pictures offers no inducement for improvement in quality.

It is a temporary provision offered and will endure only where the industry is faced with legislation and litigation, and as practiced now is so hemmed in with numerous restrictions as to be worthless.[14]

An additional alternative to straight block booking is contained in the recent consent decree signed by the five affiliated companies. It is agreed in the decree that these companies, for a limited period after August 31, 1941, will sell their features in groups of not more than five each, and the purchase of any one group will not be made contingent on the purchase of any other group. Provision is also made for the cancelation of any feature considered offensive on "moral, religious or racial grounds." The consent decree is discussed in full in appendix III.

It may be mentioned that the affiliated companies in buying each other's pictures are not, on the whole, troubled by the compulsory aspects of block booking. Instead, these companies usually negotiate selective contracts with each other. Under this system a company may contract for all the pictures distributed by another company, but retain the option of accepting for use only those which are later considered desirable. Continuity of film supply—a very desirable feature—is thus assured. At the same time, the affiliated companies acting as exhibitors assume no obligation to show films which after a preview are considered unsatisfactory.[15]

Forcing of short subjects.—Another aspect of block booking, though it is usually treated as a separate practice, is the forcing of short subjects—news reels, comedies, travelogues, etc. Short subjects are presumably used to complement features in filling out a program. Exhibitors allege that not only must they in many cases contract for

---

[13] Ibid., pp. 407–408. Letters on pp. 408–409. A similar case on pp. 261–265.
[14] Ibid., Testimony Nathan Yamins, p. 441.
[15] The selective contract not only substitutes for block booking so far as the affiliated exhibitor is concerned; it also has certain unsatisfactory connotations in connection with the delay of play dates in independent theaters. This side of the question will be discussed in a later section.

all the feature pictures offered by a single company in order to secure any; they must in addition agree to pay for and show all short subjects released by the same company.

Forcing of shorts is vigorously attacked by independent exhibitors. They contend that shorts are dated to theaters without regard to their suitability with the features shown.   Moreover, as a consequence of having to book with several distributors, exhibitors contend that they are frequently obliged to book a greater number of shorts than they require to round out their programs.   In some cases, this results in several news reels being shown simultaneously.   Even if short subjects are not shown, the exhibitor must pay for them.   Failure to pay for shorts may result in the shutting off of all film supplies.

For example, in one of Paramount's short-feature exhibition contracts 85 short subjects, exclusive of news reels, are offered.

Beginning with the first play date thereof * * * but subject to the availability of the respective one reel motion pictures licensed hereunder, the Exhibitor agrees to exhibit seven (7) one reel motion pictures each month, until the completion of the exhibition thereof.   The total license fees payable for the one reel motion pictures licensed hereunder is the sum of $255.50, which total sum the Exhibitor agrees to pay in 51 consecutive weekly installments. * * * It is agreed that the Distributor may at its option deliver to the Exhibitor c. o. d. any motion picture deliverable hereunder, and may add to said c. o. d. the amount of any past due indebtedness owing under this or any other agreement by the Exhibitor to the Distributor.[16]

Independent producers oppose the forcing of short subjects for practically the same reasons they oppose block booking.   The principal objection is that the market is closed to them through preemption of playing time.

The practice is defended by the producer-distributors on the grounds that it eliminates waste in selling expense and that the common sale of shorts and features results in savings to exhibitors.   They also claim that from their background of experience they are at least in some cases better able to judge what constitutes a well-balanced motion picture program.   It is sometimes contended that the practice was born from the desire to provide appropriate shorts to complement the showing of their features, thereby encouraging greater theater attendance.

An additional reason why the practice is favored by the producer-distributors is one less frequently advanced by them.   The short subject in some cases provides a try-out for talent which may prove suitable at some later period for use in feature pictures.   Stock short subjects also constitute a relatively inexpensive training ground for directors and technicians.   The cost of these beginners' efforts is then at least partly defrayed by booking the shorts into independent theaters.

It may be pointed out that in the operation of their own theaters the affiliated companies have in general worked out mutually satisfactory arrangements providing for selection of short subjects.   This parallels the selective contract arrangement with respect to features.

To the consumer the exact suitability of short subject material for use with particular feature pictures is probably not of great moment. It does appear, however, that the exhibitor, in direct contact with his audiences, should be in a better position to judge this factor.   The consumer is not indifferent, however, to the contention that more shorts than are necessary may be forced on the exhibitor.   If more

16 Hearings, House of Representatives, on S. 280, p. 249.

are booked than shown, the consumer is required to pay for something he does not get, since his purchase of tickets must support the process. The alternative is sometimes no more desirable. The consumer who goes to the theater to see a certain feature and then sits through a number of shorts and several dated news reels is pardonably bored or irritated. It may also be pointed out that some of the shorts which reach the screen do not tend to make the consumer appreciate the advantages of using these one- and two-reel subjects for try-outs and training.

Forcing of shorts, when accompanied by block booking, is equivalent to full-line forcing. Orders of the Federal Trade Commission, enforced by the courts, have held full-line forcing to be an unfair trade practice. In the 1927 trade practice conferences conducted by the Federal Trade Commission it was agreed that shorts should not be forced. However, no change in industry practice followed these conferences, either because of the Commission's inability to enforce its rulings, or because of difficulty in proving the compulsory nature of the practice.

Another effort to eliminate the practice was made under the N. R. A. Code of Fair Competition for the industry:

> No Distributor shall require as a condition of entering into a contract for the licensing of the exhibition of feature motion pictures that the Exhibitor contract also· for the licensing of the exhibition of a greater number of short subjects (excepting newsreels), in proportion to the total number of short subjects required by such Exhibitor, than the proportion of the feature pictures for which a contract is negotiated bears to the total number of feature pictures required by the exhibitor.[17]

This provision was criticized as making possible the forcing of shorts to the full extent of an exhibitor's playing time. Moreover—

> Distributors evaded the provision by supplying short subjects on a weekly program basis, charging the exhibitor a sum equal to an average of the payments made during the previous year. In effect the exhibitor paid an amount equal to his previous year's cost, even though the number of shorts might have been decreased.[18]

Another weakness of the provision, that of excepting news reels, was pointed out by the Independent Theatre Owners Association, Inc., of New York.

> The provision does not more than recognize the existence of an evil and in no way remedies the same. In the first place, it exempts newsreels from the operation of the provision and practice has shown many exhibitors over-stocked in newsreels, having been forced to purchase four or five newsreels from different companies. With respect to this type of short, the evil is even greater, since only one company's reels can be used under any circumstance, as they usually cover the same important news points.[19]

Under the recent consent decree, the five affiliated companies have agreed to abandon short subject forcing·during the period the decree is in effect (see Appendix III).

Blind selling.—A trade practice which has raised much hue and cry in recent years is blind selling (or blind buying). It is part and parcel of the block booking system.

At the beginning of the selling season, exhibitors are showered with glittering prospectuses from the several motion picture companies. These point in glowing terms to last season's successes and foretell

---

[17] National Recovery Administration, Code of Fair Competition for the Motion Picture Industry, art. V-D, Part 5.
[18] National Recovery Administration, Work Materials No. 34, 1936, p. 100.
[19] Hearings before Senate Finance Committee, Investigation of National Recovery Administration, 74th Cong., 1st sess., pursuant to S. Res. 79, p. 1320.

the even greater achievements to come. The exhibition contract, however, contains only what is known as a schedule of contract. A few pictures which have been completed or are nearly complete may be listed on this schedule. Several may be described as containing some particular star or featured player. The stories from which several others are to be made may be given. However, many of the pictures and in some cases all of them may be designated only by a number and a note as to the price class in which they are to fall. In accepting the contract for the block of pictures, the exhibitor in general knows no more than that he will get a certain number of pictures and that these pictures will fall in certain price classifications.

Following the schedule of contract is a paragraph which illustrates how blind selling is effected.

It is expressly understood and agreed that the Distributor does not license hereunder to the exhibitor any particular motion picture but only those motion pictures are licensed hereunder which shall be generally released by the Distributor as provided in the schedule above; that the announcement book, work sheet, press sheet, or any other announcement issued by the Distributor is issued for the purpose only of indicating what the Distributor plans to produce and does not constitute any warranty or representation that the motion pictures therein referred to or described will be generally released during the period provided in the Schedule.[20]

As indicated above, then, a few pictures are highlighted, some idea of the plots, names of stars, directors, or other attractive points being mentioned. On the whole, however, this is limited to a few top pictures. Then a disclaimer is included which relieves the distributor from the necessity of complying with his statements. It follows that the exhibitors must buy largely upon the reputation and past performance of a particular distributor's product. In effect, insofar as the independent exhibitors are concerned, it can be categorically stated that this is the only industry in which the buyer, having no idea of what he is buying, underwrites blindly all the product offered him.

The objections of independent exhibitors to blind selling are similar to their objections to block booking. The necessity of buying pictures sight unseen prevents the exhibitor from selecting out of all those features eventually released the particular ones he might consider to be most suitable for showing in his theater. As has been previously indicated, affiliated theaters have solved the problem through the device of the selective contract.

It is understandable that in selling films under the present system the actual productions sometimes fail to measure up to pre-season announcements. From this factor have arisen many complaints by independent exhibitors against distributors.

Blind selling has consistently been opposed by organizations interested in improving the moral standards of film entertainment. These groups have found that blind selling, combined with block booking, has prevented them from bringing pressure on the local exhibitor to permit some form of community selection of pictures.

The consumer standpoint on blind selling parallels that of the independent exhibitor. Any limitations on the ability of an exhibitor to license and show the best available productions and especially any restriction making it necessary to show undesirable pictures is to the consumer's disadvantage.

---

[20] Hearings, House of Representatives, pursuant to S. 280, Paramount schedule, p. 235.

The proposed remedies to blind selling have included use of the cancelation privilege. It is assumed that, in order to maintain his position in the industry, each producer will attempt to maintain a generally high standard of quality in his releases. Occasional failures are presumably taken care of through cancelation. The weakness in this system has already been indicated.

Once having secured an exhibition contract, it is to the distributor's interest to reduce cancelations to a minimum. The various means of discouraging use of the cancelation privilege, even where this has been granted by contract, go far beyond simply writing letters extolling the drawing power of the film which the exhibitor desires to cancel. This is especially so in the case of the small independent exhibitor who may have experienced difficulties in assuring himself of a continuous film supply.

An alternative proposal has been that each film included in an exhibition contract be fully described as to players, story, director, and essential situations. Such a proposal is usually accompanied by some prohibition against compulsory block booking to insure that the exhibitor may first select only those pictures he wants and then be sure of getting those pictures and no others. This is the remedy proposed in section 4 of the Neely bill.

It shall be unlawful for any distributor of motion-picture films in commerce to lease or offer to lease for public exhibition any motion-picture film or films over two thousand feet in length unless such distributor shall furnish the exhibitor at or before the time of making such lease or offer to lease an accurate synopsis of the contents of such film. Such synopsis shall be made a part of the lease and shall include (a) a general outline of the story and descriptions of the principal characters, and (b) a statement describing the manner of treatment of dialogs concerning any scenes depicting vice, crime, or suggestion of sexual passion. It is the purpose of this section to make available to the exhibitor sufficient information concerning the type and contents of the film and the manner of treatment of questionable subject matter to enable him to determine whether the film is fairly described by the synopsis.[21]

Some difficulty might arise here through lack of agreement as to what constituted an accurate synopsis. The interpretations brought out in the House and Senate committee hearings afford a glimpse of the misunderstandings and litigation which might result from such a provision. Beyond this, however, it must be recognized that if the principle of sale in advance of production is to be continued, some flexibility in description is probably desirable from the consumer standpoint. It is quite possible that unsuspected weaknesses in a scenario may develop during production or even after a preview showing. It is probably undesirable to make correction of such weaknesses contingent, among other things, on the possibility of noncompliance with contract agreements.

Finally, it has been suggested that distributors be required to trade show or preview each picture before making any exhibition contracts. Here also it is evident that some provisions regarding block booking are necessary. It would avail the exhibitor little to have a report on the film shown if he was required to contract for it regardless of his opinion as to its desirability.

Prescreening or trade showing has always been opposed by the affiliated interests. It has been their claim that prescreening would result in serious dislocations in their long-established methods of doing

[21] S. 280, 76th Cong., 3d sess.

business and would impose on them additional financial burdens. It is, therefore, interesting to note that the subject of blind selling is disposed of in the recent consent decree by provision for prescreening of all feature pictures. Assent to this provision by the five affiliated companies marks a complete reversal of their former position.[22]

We have considered various aspects of the practices of block booking, blind selling and forcing of short subjects. One fact stands out in each case. It is that each of these practices is unequally applied. So far as the affiliated interests themselves are concerned, a satisfactory answer to the problems created by the industry's selling system has been found. Insistence on any one of these practices by one of the affiliated companies in its relations with another would invite retaliation. Since the companies are generally not in competition with each other in the exhibition field, it has been found mutually more profitable to extend to each other the privilege of selection.

The three satellite producer-distributors are perforce required to grant preferential treatment in the matter of selection to the five affiliated companies. Their continued existence depends in no small part on their ability to show their pictures in the important theaters controlled by the affiliated companies.

Those who have felt the weight of block booking, blind selling and the forcing of shorts have been in the main the independent exhibitors. The very fact that the unsatisfactory features of these practices have been avoided by the dominant elements within the industry and have remained to affect, over many years, those outside the controlling group suggests very strongly the basic cause of discord. In the final analysis, the difficulty does not inherently lie in the particular method of selling which happens to be in vogue. Rather, it rests in the control exercised by the few large integrated companies over the feature films on which the industry depends for its existence.

To see this more clearly, let us create an imaginary situation. Instead of 8 large producer-distributors marketing an average of about 50 pictures each, let us suppose that there are 50 separate producer-distributors, each marketing about 8 pictures. In this hypothetical situation the number of features produced each year is roughly the same as at present. How long under such circumstances would one of these small producers remain in business if he tried to foist unsatisfactory features, at a fancy price, on his market in competition with other producers, each striving for a share of the business? Reflection reveals that the undesirable features of the present system of film sales are indissolubly connected with the high degree of control by a few companies which exists in the motion-picture industry today.

It has been contended that any change in the present system of marketing of films would result in financial losses to the major producer-distributors. This argument has been advanced by these companies themselves as a reason why various legislative remedies affecting these practices should not be enacted. It is quite evident that if pictures were not sold in blocks but were sold according to merit, severe losses might be incurred on unpopular pictures. Yet, there is no enterprise that would long stay in business if the goods offered for sale were not liked by the consumer. There can be no good reason why the motion picture industry should prove an exception in this respect.

---

[22] The provisions of the consent decree are discussed in detail in appendix III.

Dr. A. Lawrence Lowell of Harvard University, when refusing to accept an appointment on the Code Authority for the motion picture industry under the National Recovery Administration, stated:

* * * The five large producing companies have, by their business methods, obtained a controlling grip upon the business and are able to put forth upon the community any films that they please.[23]

The remedy for this situation was succintly stated in 1935 by Mr. Walter Lippmann.

Effective reform depends * * * on a clear understanding of what, given the American traditions of freedom and the variety of American tastes and American moral standards, reform ought to aim at. I would rest reform of the movies on this basic principle: That audiences shall have greater freedom to choose their pictures and that artists and producers shall have greater freedom to make pictures. * * * the best regulation would be that exercised by the customers at the box office of a theater. The best way to improve the movies would be to open the door to intense competition by independent and experimenting producers.

If the customers had freedom of choice, each community would be able to enforce the moral standards it believes in. Each exhibitor would have to take the business risk of estimating correctly the tastes of his customers * * * This is the system under which theaters, books, magazines, and newspapers operate and it is not an unsatisfactory system. Anyone, who can find a little capital, can produce what he chooses. But then he has to submit his production to the test of circulation. The highbrow and the lowbrow, the libertine and the puritan, tend to find their own audiences.[24]

DESIGNATED PLAY DATES

Through block booking and forcing of short subjects and other features, the producer-distributors have assured themselves a steady market for their product. But a steady market in itself is not enough. Along with steadiness must go profitableness. And this has in part been effected through the practice of designating play dates.

The amount of film rental to be paid for a picture may be specified in several different ways. It may be agreed that a definite flat fee will be charged for a particular showing. In another case, the distributor may accept as his rental a proportion of the box-office receipts taken in during the exhibition of a picture. Alternatively, some combination of these methods may be employed. In the usual small-theater agreement most of the features are licensed on a flat rental basis, but it is usually specified that some of the pictures, those considered likely to be the best box-office attractions, shall be paid for on a percentage basis.

All days of the week do not bring the same revenue to the box office. Attendance is greater on weekends and holidays, and admission prices are commonly higher at such times. The following table illustrates how various days of the week are usually judged from their potential box-office standpoint.[24a]

	Percent		Percent
Monday	10	Saturday	20
Tuesday	10	Sunday	25
Wednesday	10		
Thursday	10		
Friday	15	Total	100

[23] National Recovery Administration, Work Materials No. 34, p. 80.
[24] New York Herald Tribune, January 12, 1935.
[24a] Bureau of Foreign and Domestic Commerce, Department of Commerce, Motion Pictures Abroad, March 15, 1940.

Because of these differences, distributors are interested in seeing that percentage pictures play on those days of the week when box-office returns are likely to be greater.   This is accomplished by designating that the percentage pictures shall be exhibited on holidays or weekends.

The small exhibitor frequently opposes this practice.   Primarily, he objects to any restriction which keeps him from operating his theater as he pleases.   In some cases, the small theater operator would prefer to use a less satisfactory picture on a weekend, knowing that in any case attendance is likely to be satisfactory at that time, and use a stronger drawing attraction to bolster midweek returns.   The practice may maximize the distributor's revenue without performing a like function for the exhibitor.

Consumer interest in the practice of designating play dates is probably small.   Where an exhibitor shows the more desirable pictures in midweek, the consumer, who usually has less leisure at that time, may find that his interests lie parallel to those of the distributor. On the other hand, control of play dates by distributors may result, for example, in weekend bookings for sophisticated features in a theater whose audiences in the aggregate may prefer films more suited for general family entertainment.

The ability to designate play dates is another indication of the large distributors' control over the sources of supply of the industry and of the unequal bargaining strength of exhibitors and distributors.

On the whole, however, the practice is primarily an industry rather than a consumer problem.

OTHER PRACTICES AFFECTING DISTRIBUTOR-EXHIBITOR RELATIONSHIPS

The practices discussed up to this point by no means exhaust all sources of friction between distributors and exhibitors.   A minor one which may be mentioned is the practice of making score charges. The score charge is a fossillized remnant of the pre-sound days of the industry.   Before the development of sound, distributors usually supplied with each film an appropriate musical accompaniment.   The fee charged for this service was known as a score charge.   In the first sound films, the sound was supplied by discs which were played in synchronization with the film, and the score charge was attached to these disks.   Today, sound is recorded directly on the film.   Nevertheless, distributors continue in many cases to make a score charge. This irritating and apparently useless appendage of an earlier era serves constantly to annoy exhibitors who find this extra charge in their license agreements.

More important in point of distributor-exhibitor relationships is a practice charged to affiliated distributors by independent exhibitors. It has been alleged that exhibitors have been coerced into paying higher film rentals or into relinquishing an interest in a profitable theater by threats that the distributor would build or acquire a competing theater.   Such a threat is powerful indeed, since the independent exhibitor is well aware that a competing affiliated theater will usually receive a choice of the available pictures by virtue of the cooperative arrangements existing between the major companies.

In this field it is difficult to distinguish between the operations of the affiliated company as an exhibitor or as a distributor.   Powerful independent theater chains have found the means to enter localities and take over the businesses of competing exhibitors by means which will be subsequently discussed. The exact method whereby a similar result has been achieved by an affiliated company is sometimes difficult to ascertain. The possibilities are illustrated by a contempt citation against the Fox West Coast Theatres Corporation—the exhibition branch of the Twentieth Century-Fox organization. This charge states:

> As a result of the practices and activities described in this Petition and Information, many unaffiliated exhibitors in the Los Angeles Exchange Territory have been unable either to contract for first or second run or first suburban run pictures, or to contract for pictures to exhibit in competition with defendant Fox West Coast, and therefore have been impelled either to sell their theaters outright to Fox West Coast, or to enter into profit-sharing agreements, or pooling arrangements, so-called, under which the unaffiliated exhibitor has granted Fox West Coast a controlling interest in his theater or has pooled the theater with a theater operated by defendant Fox West Coast, which receives an equal or controlling interest in the venture.[25]

The charge then names 26 unaffiliated theaters which were turned over to Fox West Coast or pooled with its theaters between 1932 and 1936.

While it is quite true that a similar result might have been achieved by a powerful independent exhibition chain, it is nevertheless reasonable to assume that the affiliation of the exhibition organization with one of the major producers was no hindrance to these activities.

The Code of Fair Competition for the Motion Picture Industry, promulgated under the N. R. A., declared it to be an unfair trade practice for any distributor to threaten, coerce or intimidate any exhibitor into entering a contract for the exhibition of motion pictures or into paying higher film rentals by the commission of any overt act evidencing an intention to build or acquire a competing theater.[26] It was added, however, that this should in no way abrogate the right of a producer or distributor to build or acquire in good faith a theater in any location. The effect of this proviso was to nullify the entire clause, since it was incumbent on the aggrieved party to prove the act was not in good faith.

That both of these practices—making score charges and coercion of exhibitors into entering film contracts, into paying higher film rentals or into relinquishing control of their theaters—still constitute sources of discord in the industry is seen from the fact that these practices are included among the charges made by the Government against the major companies in the recent antitrust suit.[27] The consent decree recently entered as a result of this suit, however, contains no stipulation with respect to either of these practices.

OVERBUYING

Overbuying of films is a practice whereby an exhibitor licenses more features than are strictly necessary for the operation of a theater, with the express intention of preventing a competitor from securing enough good pictures to permit normal operations. It is a constant threat to the small exhibitor competing with a powerful opponent.

[25] *United States of America* v. *Fox West Coast Theaters Corporation, et al.*, in the District Court of the United States for the Southern District of California, Central Division, information charging criminal contempt and petition for rule to show cause, No. 14048-C, filed Aug. 31, 1939.
[26] National Recovery Administration, Code of Fair Competition for the Motion Picture Industry, art. V, division D, Part 1 of the approved code, 1933.
[27] *United States* v. *Paramount, Inc.*, 1940.

The fear aroused by this practice may be judged from the fact that about 85 percent of the complaints submitted to the N. R. A. before formulation of the code for the motion picture industry dealt with some form of overbuying.[28]

Overbuying manifests itself in many ways. In its simplest form, an exhibitor buys more pictures than he can use, simply to prevent their use by a competitor. Overbuying may also take the form of unnecessary and too frequent changes of program which, as in the first instance, results in a shortage of films available to competing exhibitors. In still another form, an exhibitor, as a condition to entering into a contract, may require that a distributor refrain from licensing pictures to a competitor. Such an agreement, which gives the exhibitor sole exhibition rights in his locality, is known as an "exclusive rights" contract.

The effect of overbuying on the consumer is so obvious that it hardly needs to be depicted. In the first place, if the number of operating theaters is actually reduced, there is an economic loss to the community, since no new enterprise enters the field to take the place of that deposed. The practice may result in the absolute reduction of the number of films shown in the locality where an exhibitor makes them unavailable to a competitor but does not use them himself.

As an alternative to this practice, the offending exhibitor sometimes attempts to show the pictures by resorting to a policy of frequent changes of program. This not only limits the consumer in his choice of a place and a time to see particular films. It may mean complete loss of opportunity to see particular features since in the localities in which overbuying is most common, a feature is seldom shown more than once.

Finally, if the practice succeeds in its objective of eliminating all competition, the protection afforded to the consumer by this competition is wholly lost. The consumer remains with only the choice of seeing pictures on terms offered by the exhibitor or not seeing them at all.

Overbuying, when undertaken with the express purpose of eliminating competition, is almost certainly a violation of the Federal antitrust statutes. Consequently, a number of complaints against overbuying have from time to time been filed in the Federal courts. A case pending at the present time may be used to illustrate the general tenor of such suits.[29]

The complainant states that he started operating the Palace Theater in St. Johnsbury, Vt., in the fall of 1926. Shortly after, another independent, the Star Theater, was opened in the same town. Both theaters operated on a policy of 3 to 4 films weekly, and each secured about one-half of all the major distributors' product. For profitable operation each theater needed approximately 200 films annually.

In August 1935, the Interstate Theater Corporation, an extensive New England chain, leased the Star through a subsidiary. The operator of the Palace alleges that Interstate then made contracts with the major distributors whereby the Star was granted special privileges, including price concessions, priority in play dates, rights of selection of pictures and cancelation privileges, and that due to the strong bargaining power of Interstate, the major distributors refused to license

[28] National Recovery Administration, Work Materials No. 34, p. 70.
[29] *Tegu's Palace Theatre, Inc.* V. *Interstate Theatre Corporation, et al.*, Civil Action No. 25, District Court of the United States, District of Vermont.

quality films to the Palace Theater. Finally, the operator of the Palace claims that in the fall of 1935 Interstate changed the operating policy of the Star Theater from showing 3 or 4 pictures weekly to approximately 6, thus absorbing most of the desirable films produced. The complainant asks an injunction against the continuance of the alleged discrimination and liquidated damages to the extent of three times the loss he has suffered.

The failure of the antitrust statutes completely to check overbuying perhaps lies primarily in the difficulty of determining whether in any particular instance contracts are made with the express intention of eliminating competition or simply as a normal consequence of competitive conditions.

The Code of Fair Competition for the Motion Picture Industry recognized the existence of the practice and incorporated a provision expressly forbidding overbuying in any form, no matter how accomplished.[30] Moreover, it was a function of the 31 grievance boards set up under the code in the different exchange areas to hear complaints with respect to overbuying and to grant affirmative relief in cases where the practice had been used. These grievance boards, set up shortly after the code became operative on December 7, 1933, reported that 164 overbuying cases had been considered by April 1, 1935. While exact information is not available, it is known that overbuying was found to have existed in a number of cases.

Overbuying is usually found only in the smaller communities. The primary objective of the practice is to stifle and, if possible, to eliminate competition by preempting the film supply. This is generally possible only when the number of competing theaters in the area is small. In the larger communities, a picture will usually sustain several showings, and the exhibitor unable to secure pictures on some preferred run, may generally show them at a later date and at a lower admission price. In such situations, the powerful exhibitor may use selective contracts, extended clearance, or unfairly specified admission prices (q. v.) to restrict the opportunities of smaller competitors.

There is an even more necessary limitation on the use of overbuying. The exhibitor resorting to the practice must by some means secure the cooperation of the important distributors—not a few of them but all or nearly all. It follows that these distributors must be offered some consideration of greater importance to them than the rentals which might be paid by the theater unable to secure films. This requirement will seldom, if ever, be fulfilled where two exhibitors compete on relatively even terms; the overbuying exhibitor is nearly always found to be operating a chain of theaters. Each distributor is moved to cooperate by the threat that failure to assist in the disestablishment of the exhibitor against whom the practice is to be used will be followed by a boycott of the distributor's films in some of the chain's theaters, with a consequent loss in revenue. Where two affiliated companies are involved, the promise of mutual assistance in similar situations may also be a factor.

The intent of overbuying is to achieve a local monopoly in the exhibition of pictures by eliminating all competition. To attain this end, the buying power of large numbers of theaters, located perhaps

---

[30] National Recovery Administration, Code of Fair Competition for the Motion Picture Industry, art. VI, Part 2, sec. 1 of the approved code.

in many States, is brought to bear on a single local competitive situation. Overbuying may be practiced by a large independent theater organization, but an affiliated theater has an additional advantage in that it can usually count on the cooperation of the other large distributors. The practice is clearly a manifestation of the power of the large bargaining unit in the exhibition field.

SELECTIVE CONTRACTS

Results similar to overbuying are achieved in large cities through selective contracts. By means of this device, the large exhibitor may contract for all the pictures released by a distributor, but obligate himself to use and pay for only a part of these. The features to be used are selected after release, and after the pictures have been tested for box-office value. Under these contracts the large exhibitor is also allowed extended playing time on hit pictures, which tends to make his requirements unpredictable. Nor are rejected pictures made available to competing exhibitors soon after national release. Instead, selection may be delayed so as to hold up exhibition of pictures in competing theaters. Since much of the value of pictures depends on their timeliness, this may operate alike to the disadvantage of competing exhibitors, consumers, and the cooperating distributors.

Use of selective contracts as an unfair competitive device was recognized in the N. R. A. code for the industry. A provision of the code required that pictures bought on a selective basis be accepted or rejected within 21 days after their availability in the exhibition territory where the theater was located was announced by the distributor.[31]

The effects of selective contracts may be illustrated in Chicago, where the Balaban and Katz theater chain, affiliated with Paramount, dominates the exhibition field. In the 3-year period from November 1935 to November 1938, Balaban and Katz had exclusive choice of all features released by Loew's, Warner's, Paramount, and Fox for first-run exhibition in its "Loop" theaters. These companies released a total of 670 features in this interval, exclusive of reissues, and of these only 388 were shown by Balaban and Katz in the "Loop" theaters. During the same period, United Artist's released 57 features, 47 were licensed by Balaban and Katz, and 40 were shown in these houses.[32]

The control by Balaban and Katz of the product of four of the five major companies resulted in a delay in the first showing of many pictures until they could conveniently be booked into one of the "Loop" theaters. Motion picture patrons in Chicago thus had their first opportunity to attend many popular features more than two months after the pictures had been nationally released.[33] Because of the prior playing position of the Balaban and Katz "Loop" theaters, these delays were likewise forced upon the customers of all theaters in the entire Chicago exchange area.

[31] Ibid., art. V, division E, Part 1.
[32] *United States* v. *Balaban, et al.*, criminal action No. 31,230, in the District Court of the United States for the Northern District of Illinois, Eastern Division, proposed findings of fact submitted on behalf of the Government, p. 50. During this period R-K-O and Universal features were shown in a first-run theater operated by R-K-O.
[33] Among many, these features were first shown in Chicago the following number of days after national release: "Tovarich," 68 days; "Rembrandt," 63 days; "Topper," 60 days; "Captains Courageous," 56 days; "A Night at the Opera," 60 days.

CLEARANCE AND ZONING

In the early days of the industry (as pointed out in ch. I) distributors made a number of prints of each film and sold them outright to exhibitors. The prints were released for simultaneous exhibition in a number of theaters in the same territory. It was soon discovered that consecutive showing of films by the several exhibitors in a competitive situation was more economical and this method of distribution became general.

Since the potential market of the first exhibitor of a film was the greatest, a higher rental fee was asked for the earlier showings. In consideration of the higher rental paid, a prior run exhibitor was granted "protection" over competing theaters. This consisted of a stipulation that no competing theaters should show the same film until a specified period of time had elapsed after the completion of the particular showing licensed. This period of time came to be known as "clearance." The term "zoning" was adopted to designate the area over which clearance was effective, and "run" to indicate a theater's playing position. The theater first showing films in a zone is known as the first-run theater. Correspondingly, there are second-run theaters, third-run, and so on.

In the early stages of development, clearance systems were far from uniform. The protection and run enjoyed by an exhibitor might vary with the identity of the distributor from whom films were licensed. Largely by trial and error, clearance arrangements began to fall into a pattern in which each theater occupied a definite place. Today, a theater usually negotiates similar run and protection terms from each distributor that supplies him with films.

The establishment of clearance schedules is an intricate procedure. It involves a complex bargaining process and the balance of a variety of opposing economic interests. It may be stated initially that the primary objective of the distributor is, of course, to maximize his total revenue from each picture. This aim gives him a very direct interest in clearance periods. The higher rental fees paid by the prior-run exhibitor are directly conditioned on the extent of the protection which he is granted, and in general the longer the clearance period before subsequent showing, the higher the rental fee the prior-run exhibitor will pay.

On the other hand, the distributor's revenue from subsequent-run exhibition is also important to him; this income may mean the difference between black or red ink on his ledgers. But the longer the clearance period, the smaller will be these returns—not only because more customers will have attended the prior showing rather than wait for subsequent exhibition, but also because the effects of the advertising and exploitation efforts made when the picture was released will have been vitiated over this time. In general, the greater the total box-office return earned by a film in all showings, the greater will be the distributor's revenue.

Opposed to the distributor in the bargaining processes are the theater operators in a particular competitive location. The first factor to be settled is the run enjoyed by a particular theater. This is primarily determined by the amount of sales which the theater can be expected to make. This in turn is a function of the theater's seating capacity, its location, the newness and desirability of its facilities, and the admission prices which it can charge. First-run showings are usually booked into the theaters having the largest potential box-office receipts, since such theaters can pay the highest film rentals. Such theaters are, of course, the largest houses centrally located in cities so as to draw audiences from an entire metropolitan area.

The objective of the operator of a first-run theater is to bargain for as much protection over subsequent showings as possible since in this way he tends to increase his total revenues. The length of the clearance period must, however, be balanced against the higher film rentals which will be charged by the distributor for extended protection. The operator of a subsequent-run theater may have to consider not only the protection over still later showings, but also his position with respect to prior exhibition.

The admission price charged by a theater is always an important element in setting clearance periods. It is the universal practice for the distributor to stipulate in each exhibition contract the minimum admission price at which films may be shown. This is not done simply to protect the distributor's interest in pictures which may be licensed on percentage terms. Customarily, each subsequent showing of a film in a competitive area is made at a lower admission price. The subsequent sale value of a film may, therefore, in large part be determined by the admission prices which have been charged in the prior-run theaters.

The relation between clearance and admission is quite flexible. In general, the higher the admission price charged by any particular exhibitor, the longer the clearance period which will be granted by the distributor. Conversely, admission prices can generally be reduced only at the expense of less satisfactory protection terms. Clearance and admission prices can thus not be considered separately. It may well be that the location of a theater will determine the admission prices which it can charge, and this in turn will fix the theater's clearance period.

The complex bargaining involved makes the establishment of clearance schedules difficult indeed, but these difficulties rise almost wholly in urban areas. Clearance presents few problems in small towns or isolated areas where not more than two or three theaters are in direct competition. Such theaters may play behind the prior-run houses in the large cities, but this is not likely materially to affect their revenues. Moreover, even in the large cities, it is the establishment of equitable clearance periods between the first-run and subsequent-run theaters which is most difficult. The longest clearance period is usually set between the first showing of a film in the large downtown theaters and any subsequent showing. Clearance between subsequent runs is frequently quite brief.

The relation between run, clearance and zoning, admission price, seating capacity, and rental fees is indeed a complex one. The range covered by these factors is indicated by this fact: a license fee amounting to many thousands of dollars may be paid for the first showing of a film in a large metropolitan theater, and within a year the same film may be exhibited in some small theater in the same city for a fee of less than $20.

A further indication is given by the experience of the feature "Gone With the Wind." This picture was released early in 1940 for showing at substantially advanced admission prices. At this time it was advertised that the film would not be shown again at lower prices before 1941. Nevertheless, despite the advanced admission prices, public interest in the picture was so great that record-breaking numbers of persons paid $1 or more each rather than wait until the film was available at a lower figure. It is reported that the receipts from this single showing at advanced prices more than covered the entire production and exploitation costs of the picture, though these were large. Because of the high admission prices originally charged, the picture will continue to bring in revenue for some time to come. Nor will admission prices soon be reduced to those usually charged for subsequent-run showing. It may be parenthetically noted that the rental fees charged exhibitors for this showing were likewise record-breaking in many instances. This case is an unusual one, but it nevertheless indicates the important relationship between clearance, admission price, and film rentals.

In the idealized situation where all the elements of the industry are in active competition with one another, the clearance pattern resulting may be considered to come from a balancing of the conflicting objectives of each of the elements. A clearance system of this type probably represents the best method for distribution of motion pictures which could be devised. It permits the distribution of films both rapidly and economically. Moreover, the resulting exhibition pattern is relatively stable, in itself an advantage to the consumer. But, like many other systems which in an economic sense may be basically sound, the clearance system is subject to abuse by dominating elements within the industry.

Powerful exhibition interests competing with weaker rivals have demanded extended clearance periods from distributors, and have insisted that they be granted protection over geographical areas larger than could be warranted in any economic sense. In view of the larger aggregate rentals paid by these dominating exhibition units as compared with their smaller competitors, and the fear that these rentals might be reduced or withdrawn, distributors in many cases have acquiesced to these demands.

The primary reason for the negotiation of extended protection has been, of course, the simple desire to hear the cheery ring of the bell in the cash register. A theater able to negotiate extended clearance without being required to pay correspondingly higher rentals tends to draw patronage away from competing subsequent-run exhibitors. That this practice may render the competitor's business wholly unprofitable may not be an undesirable aspect of the situation. If the large exhibitor is able to acquire cheaply the properties of his competitors, he may achieve a local monopoly of the exhibition field. In this case the admission prices and clearance periods which are established will be designed solely to enhance his profits at the expense of all motion picture patrons in the locality, so far as this may be permitted by the distributors.

The consumer interest in unfair clearance is quite clear. The consumer desires to see each picture as promptly as possible and at the lowest admission price compatible with continued desirable service. It is quite evident that unfair clearance, whether present as such or carried through to the ultimate objective of a local monopoly, directly contravenes the interests of the consumer.

Unfair clearance is not primarily a question of producer-distributor control of exhibition. It has been employed repeatedly by large independent theater organizations. Nevertheless, the practice has been closely identified with the theater operations of the major companies. As has been already indicated, the five major companies control and operate a great number of large prior-run theaters throughout the United States. Since unfair clearance is most usually instituted by such theaters over subsequent-run competitors, this control is most significant. Moreover, since these major companies in general do not compete with each other in their theater operation activities, the mutual advantages to be derived from reciprocal permission to enforce unfair protection terms on subsequent-run exhibitors must not be disregarded.

Indicative of the different types of situations which may develop contingent upon the control of theaters by one of the affiliated companies is the practice with respect to clearance between first and subsequent-runs in Washington, D. C., and in Atlanta, Ga. In Washington six downtown theaters are operated by three major companies, but the majority of the neighborhood houses throughout the city are owned and operated by Warner Bros. In general, the clearance of the first-run theaters over Warner's neighborhood houses amounts to about 28 days. Obviously, in Washington it is to the advantage of Warner Bros. to arrange clearance schedules to maximize the revenue of their neighborhood theaters, so far as this does not conflict with reasonable profits in the first-run houses.

Contrasting with this, five first-run theaters are operated by two affiliated companies in Atlanta. No one of the major companies operates subsequent-run theaters in this city. The interests of the two major companies operating these first-run theaters are obviously best served by extending clearance periods so as to divert as large a share as possible of exhibition revenue into the first-run houses. The clearance period in Atlanta on first-quality pictures is in the neighborhood of 60 days or more.

Because of the disadvantageous position of the small independent exhibitor in negotiating clearance, as compared with the affiliated exhibitors and the large independent circuits, unfair clearance has become one of the most frequent and the most serious complaints by independent exhibitors. There has indeed been a strong basis for their claims. Where they have been subject to unfair protection restrictions, their profits have soon become losses. More than one exhibitor has seen his theater investment depreciated in value until he decided the only thing to do was to close its doors. Practically every legal action filed by an independent exhibitor or by the Government against an affiliated company or an independent theater circuit has contained charges of inequitable clearance and zoning.

Peculiarly enough, the interests of the distributor without theater connections in a particular locality to some extent parallel those of the consumer and the independent exhibitor. Unfair clearance is granted by a distributor to theaters affiliated with another distributor or forming part of an independent chain not primarily to obtain increased revenues, but rather from fear of reduced revenues if he fails to comply.

Fears of loss of revenue in other B & K situations if its requirements in the loop were not met were expressed by representatives of two of these defendants [major distributors] in conversation with other exhibitors.[34]

---

[34] *United States* V. *Barney Balaban, et al.,* op. cit.

The curious conflicts of interest within the industry caused by the question of unfair protection have resulted in a queer half-conviction on the part of even those using the practice that it might be better all around if equitable clearance and zoning schedules generally applicable throughout the industry might be developed. The establishment of equitable protection arrangements, while it has an easy sound, is most difficult of attainment. Large theater investments have in many cases been made on the basis of existing clearance arrangements. The question as to whether these clearances are now equitable is likely to be considered somewhat beside the point when a change may vastly depreciate values. Nevertheless, efforts have been made by the industry to rationalize the clearance system.

Discussions which were intended to lead to uniform clearance and zoning schedules were inaugurated in about 1930 through the film boards of trade. These film boards of trade represent the local organizations of the major distributors in each of the key cities. Exhibitors and distributors conferred on the establishment of these schedules. It was intended that each theater in an exchange area would be allotted a definite playing position, and that all distributors would adhere to the schedule adopted. Uniform clearance and zoning schedules were set up for about 10 exchange areas for the 1930–31 season. However, in 1 of these territories, an independent exhibitor, feeling that the schedules discriminated against him, instituted legal action under the antitrust statutes. The court declared the plan to be illegal under the Sherman Act, and it was abandoned.[35]

The establishment of uniform schedules was again attempted under the N. R. A. Code for the Motion Picture Industry. Clearance and zoning boards, consisting of representatives of distributors and exhibitors, were set up in each of 31 exchange cities. However, only 1 major schedule was approved during the life of the code—that for the Los Angeles territory—and in this case a number of the protests were outstanding at the time of approval. Nevertheless, the local clearance and zoning boards considered 875 individual complaints of inequitable protection arrangements. and in many of these relief was ordered.

No further attempts to set up uniform schedules have been made since invalidation of the code. However, it must be noted that existing protection arrangements with respect to any theater are substantially the same for all major distributors.

The subject of unfair clearance is recognized in section VIII of the recent consent decree signed by the five major companies. It is stipulated that the reasonableness of the protection applicable to an exhibitor's theater shall be subject to arbitration. With certain restrictions the question of the run to be enjoyed by a theater is also subject to arbitration under the consent decree. The provisions of the consent decree are discussed in greater detail in appendix III.

Presumably, the exhibitor subject to unfair clearance can bring a successful action under the antitrust laws, alleging arbitrary and concerted action to limit competition and injure his business. As in the case of overbuying, the principal difficulty is in determining whether the particular conditions obtaining have resulted from the complex economic forces involved or from an express intent to exploit unfairly the advantage of greater buying power. It must be agreed that in any particular situation, even with all the facts, it is most

---

[35] *Youngclaus* V. *Omaha Film Board of Trade*, 60F (2d) 538, July 2, 1932.

difficult to establish exactly what equitable protection should be. The consumer generally lacks such resources, and his protection from the effects of unfair clearance must come principally from the forces of competition.

The clearance developed between a number of theaters, wholly independent of affiliation with other theaters or with distributors, and competing with each other for films and protection terms, is likely to approximate the conditions most desirable from the consumer standpoint. Where none of these elements is in a position to exact unwarranted profits at the expense of his competitors or the consumer, the consumer's interests are probably well protected. It is when large numbers of theaters are joined together into a single bargaining unit that unfair clearance is likely to develop. It is apparent that the problems arising from unfair clearance and zoning, like those developing from overbuying, are almost wholly a result of large-scale combination of interests in the exhibition field.

UNFAIRLY SPECIFIED ADMISSION PRICES

As mentioned in the preceding section, minimum admission prices are specified in each exhibition contract and constitute an important feature of the license agreement. Inserted originally for the protection of the distributor, admission prices, like clearance and zoning restrictions, have in some cases been converted by strong exhibition interests into a weapon against weaker competitors. This power has resulted in the setting of minimum admission prices in the contracts of subsequent-run exhibitors at higher levels than warranted by the clearance and zoning restrictions negotiated. The effects of this practice are, of course, identical with those of unfairly extended clearance and zoning and are equally vicious from the consumer standpoint.

An interesting illustration involves the Interstate Circuit and the Texas Consolidated Theaters, both affiliated with Paramount.[36] Through ownership of about 131 theaters, about half of which are first-run theaters (there are 1,073 theaters in operation in Texas and New Mexico at present)[37] these two circuits dominate exhibition in Texas and New Mexico,[38] and have been successful in dictating to the various distributors the terms at which the latter may license films to independents.

The following letter was sent by Interstate to each of the major distributors:

GENTLEMEN: On April 25th the writer notified you that in purchasing product for the coming season 34–35, it would be necessary for all distributors to take into consideration in the sale of subsequent runs that Interstate Circuit, Inc., will not agree to purchase produce to be exhibited in its "A" theaters at a price of 40 cents or more for night admission, unless distributors agree that in selling their product to subsequent runs, that this "A" product will never be exhibited at any time or in any theater at a smaller admission price than 25 cents for adults in the evening.

In addition to this price restriction, we also request that on "A" pictures which are exhibited at a night admission price of 40 cents or more—they shall never be exhibited in conjunction with another feature picture under the so-called policy of double-features.

[36] *U. S.* v. *Interstate Circuit, Inc., et al.*, Equity No. 3736-992, 1938.
[37] 1940 Motion Picture Yearbook.
[38] Their domination in the cities where their theaters are located is indicated by the fact that at the time of the contracts in question, Interstate and Consolidated each contributed more than 74 percent of all the license fees paid by motion picture theaters in their territories. (Opinion, Supreme Court of the United States, Nos. 269, 270, p. 3.)

At this time the writer desires to again remind you of these restrictions due to the fact that there may be some delay in consummating all our feature film deals for the coming season, and it is imperative that in your negotiations that you afford us this clearance.

In the event that a. distributor sees fit to sell his product to subsequent runs in violation of this request, it definitely means that we cannot negotiate for his product to be exhibited in our "A" theaters at top admission prices.

We, naturally, in purchasing subsequent runs from the distributors in certain of our cities, must necessarily eliminate double featuring and maintain the maximum 25 cent admission price, which we are willing to do.

Right at this time the writer wishes to call your attention to the Rio Grande Valley situation. We must insist that all pictures exhibited in our "A" theaters at a maximum night admission price of 35 cents must also be restricted to subsequent runs in the Valley at 25 cents. Regardless of the number of days which may intervene, we feel that in exploiting and selling the distributors' product, that subsequent runs should be restricted to at least a 25 cent admission scale.

The writer will appreciate your acknowledging your complete understanding of this letter.

Sincerely,

(Signed)   R. J. O'DONNELL.[39]

Conferences between the Circuit and the distributors resulted in the latter's agreement to impose the restrictions outlined.

Prior to the 1934–35 season, subsequent-run exhibition contracts generally provided for a minimum admission price of 15 cents, in some cases 10 cents. The new price restrictions thus represented a large increase. In those low-income areas where the independent exhibitors could not meet the new restrictions, the members of the community were furnished with only the poorer products of the industry. The pictures denied the theaters with a lesser admission price were played at the first-run theaters with admission prices of 40 cents or more, and those patrons who formerly waited for subsequent runs could, after the change, see desirable pictures only at first-run theaters. Attendance was thus diverted from the subsequent-run theaters to Interstate's first-run theaters, and the income of the former was reduced.

How the process was viewed by an independent exhibitor in this territory, as well as the close connection between clearance and admission price, is illustrated by the following testimony at a congressional hearing.

I have here the clearance schedule for the Interstate Circuit in Texas. It is written by the Interstate people, also their affiliated Texas Consolidated, covering some of the smaller towns, and it is laid down by all of the film companies, who abide by it. It lays down the rules that they expect to have followed, regarding the clearance of their theaters * * *.

If you will notice this, there is a provision that a neighborhood theater in Dallas * * * which charges 25 cents, shall wait 90 days after the downtown first run, before it can get its picture * * *. If the charge is 20 cents, it must wait 120 days. So, there is the place where the control of prices comes in, because if I am running the 25-cent theater and elect or choose to reduce my admission price to 20. cents, I automatically force myself back 30 days further in clearance. My people must wait 4 months instead of 3 months after the picture has been shown downtown before they can see it. Naturally that affects my box office. Naturally that drives away some customers. I have to figure for myself as to whether the reduction in price will bring me more customers than the lengthening of the time, the older the age of the picture, will lose me customers * * *.[40]

This particular case is especially interesting as showing that one of the major companies was successful in securing the cooperation of the

[39] *Interstate Circuit, Inc., et al.* V. *The United States Of America* (No. 269), appeals from the District Court of the United States for the Northern District of Texas, February 13, 1939.
[40] Hearings, House of Representatives, pursuant to S. 280, testimony H. A. Cole, p. 387.

other large distributors in inaugurating a radical change in practice—a change, by the way, which they felt was counter to their own best interests. Universal's branch manager, in forwarding the letter quoted above to his home office, wrote:

> I am sure this will give you some idea as to how tough these fellows expect to be in the Dallas territory, and it looks to me like a sales policy that should be "nipped in the bud" in New York for after all, a policy of this sort is extremely dangerous to everyone concerned and cannot help, in the long run, but cost us all plenty of money.

R-K-O's branch manager, in forwarding the same letter to his home office, wrote:

> In view of the fact that this letter requests us to set up a definite sales policy as outlined by them, I would appreciate your advising me if under our national sales policy, we would be within our rights to agree to any such set-up even if we agreed with them. They are automatically trying to set up a model arrangement for the United States without giving us anything to say about it.

Metro's branch manager wrote to his home office:

> In my opinion Bob is making some unfair demands, imposing conditions on us of which he is a flagrant violator. This has particular reference to the fifth paragraph of his letter, as he is playing double features in Ft. Worth, San Antonio, and plenty of other situations.[41]

The Supreme Court in its opinion found that the activities outlined were the result of an agreement which "constituted a combination and conspiracy in restraint of interstate commerce in violation of the Sherman Act."[42]

In this particular case a clear-cut decision against the practice, endorsed by the Supreme Court, was obtained. However, in this instance there was clear and incontrovertible evidence that admission prices were deliberately set to restrict competition from subsequent-run exhibitors. In many other cases it will be uncertain whether an equivalent result has not been achieved by indirect means.

Other Practices Affecting Relationships Between Exhibitors

Various means have been indicated whereby a powerful exhibitor may limit the competition of a less powerful opponent or even drive him from business. However, in many cases it may not even be necessary to use methods which tend to place the competitor's business on an unprofitable basis. The mere threat of employment of one or more of these devices where the smaller exhibitor has the certain knowledge that the power to carry out the threat is available may provide a sufficient inducement to the small exhibitor to relinquish part or all of his exhibition interests to the more powerful competitor.

Other practices may be used to the same effect. The larger exhibitor may threaten to acquire a competing theater or he may actually acquire such a theater and operate it at a loss until the smaller exhibitor is forced to meet his terms. The variety of means which

[41] U. S. v. Interstate Circuit, Inc., et al., op. cit.
[42] Interstate Circuit, Inc. v. U. S., op cit.
* * * the distributor appellants agreed and conspired among themselves to take uniform action upon the proposals made by Interstate * * * that they carried out the agreement by imposing the restrictions upon their subsequent-run licensees in those cities, causing some of them to increase their admission price to 25 cents * * * that the effect of the restrictions upon 'low-income members of the community' patronizing the theaters of these exhibitors was to withold from them altogether the 'best entertainment furnished by the motion picture industry;' and that the restrictions operated to increase the income of the distributors and of Interstate and to deflect attendance from later-run exhibitors who yielded to the restrictions to the first-run theaters of Interstate * * * The court concluded * * * the agreement * * * constituted a combination and conspiracy in restraint of interstate commerce in violation of the Sherman Act." (*Id*.)

may be employed in this type of situation are illustrated. in a complaint instituted against a powerful independent exhibitor chain. The complaint states in part:

> By reason of the control by defendant exhibitors of the most desirable motion pictures as hereinbefore set forth, defendant exhibitors have been able practically to eliminate the competition of independent exhibitors in the Crescent towns. Independent exhibitors have been induced to sell their theaters to defendant exhibitors under the threat, express or implied, that if they refused to sell, defendant exhibitors would open competing theaters in the same town and prevent the independent exhibitor from procuring desirable pictures. In a number of instances, independent exhibitors attempting to compete with defendant exhibitors have found it impossible to procure sufficient pictures to keep their theaters in operation. In addition, defendant exhibitors have lowered their prices, giving away large sums of money as prizes, and operated some of their theaters at a loss with the purpose and effect of driving their competitors out of business and giving defendant exhibitors a monopoly in the exhibition of motion pictures in the area in which they operate. By the use of such tactics defendant exhibitors have forced a large number of independent exhibitors in the States of Tennessee, Kentucky, Alabama, Mississippi, and Arkansas out of the motion-picture business and, unless restrained and enjoined by this court, will continue to do so in the future until they have complete control of the motion picture exhibition business in the area in which they operate.[43]

The bill of particulars stated, among others, 26 instances in which the chains took over or closed out small independent theaters during a period of 5 years.

A second case, while not strictly concerned with the treatment of an exhibitor by a more powerful competitor, nevertheless illustrates how domination of an exhibition territory may be used. The case concerns the Balaban & Katz Corporation, the exhibition outlet of Paramount in Chicago.

The Oriental Theatre in Chicago was constructed, as part of a larger project, expressly for first-run exhibition of motion pictures. Before the building was completed, the Balaban & Katz Corporation, on August 25, 1924, executed a lease for the building, to run for 50 years at a rental of $327,000 per year. It was specifically provided in the agreement that the lease might not be reassigned to any corporation having capital and surplus of less than $1,000,000 at the time of assignment.

On February 29, 1932, John Balaban, Barney Balaban, and Sam Katz, representing the Balaban & Katz Corporation, formed the Oriental Theatre Co. This company had a capital and surplus of $1,013,132.97, of which $1,013,020.81 consisted of accounts receivable from the Balaban & Katz Corporation. The lease for the Oriental Theatre was assigned to this corporation on March 5, 1932. Five days later the stockholders of the Oriental Theatre Co. met and declared a dividend of $903,485.21.

This maneuver was preliminary to a demand in October or November 1932 by the attorney representing both the Balaban & Katz Corporation and the Oriental Theatre Co. that the owners of the building reduce the amount of the rental for the theater. Since the Balaban & Katz Corporation controlled the Chicago exhibition field, the owners recognized the inevitable, and on December 14, 1932, agreed to a reduction in the rental to $200,000 per year. In July or August 1935 a request for a further reduction in rental was made, but this was not granted. Finally, after some intervening negotiations,

[43] United States V. Crescent Amusement Company, Inc., et al., in the District Court of the United States for the Middle District of Tennessee, Nashville division, complaint, civil action No. 54, filed August 11, 1939.

the Oriental Theatre Co. defaulted on the rent and discontinued operation of the theater on May 26, 1938. As a consequence of this action, the lease was canceled on September 22, 1938.

At this time Balaban & Katz offered to lease the theater for $125,000 per year, with a percentage of any profits made above a certain figure.[44] When this offer was refused, the owners were informed by the representatives of Balaban & Katz conducting the negotiations that they might as well lease to B. & K. since "they are the only people that can get pictures for the house." This statement appeared justified, since negotiations with a number of independent exhibitors for operation of the house were unsuccessful. After examination of the possibilities, each of these concluded that they would be unable to secure sufficient first-quality prior-run product to make the operation of the theater successful. Finally, the theater was leased to an unaffiliated exhibitor for 25 years, commencing November 1, 1938, on percentage terms with a guaranteed rental of $150,000 a year after the first 2 years.

This case was summarized by the Government as follows:

The theater was built and opened as a first-run house under B. & K. management, at a rental of $327,000 a year. After 6 years of such operation, it was assigned to a subsidiary without financial responsibility as a preliminary to negotiations which reduced the rental to $200,000 a year. B. & K. then defaulted again shortly after the new lease was made, finally closed the theater. and then offered to lease it again for $125,000 a year. B. & K. could default the lease and close the theater without having to consider the possibility of first-run competition from that theater in other hands only because it controlled the supply of first-run pictures necessary to operate that theater on the policy for which it was built. In so doing, it ruthlessly depreciated the investment represented by that theater in a manner which the owners were helpless to combat.[45]

---

[44] *United States* v. *Barney Balaban et al.*, op. cit. For purposes of comparison the figure agreed upon in the Loew 5-year franchise as the rental assigned to the Roosevelt Theatre in Chicago, owned by the B. & K. Corporation, in computing film rentals on percentage pictures was $188,295.64 per year. Seating capacity of the Oriental was 3,800 as against 1,540 for the Roosevelt.
[45] Ibid.

CHAPTER III

OBSERVATIONS

CHAPTER III

OBSERVATIONS

The production and distribution branches of the motion picture industry are dominated by five large companies. These are flanked by three satellite organizations unable in their own economic interests to oppose the policies of the controlling five.

It has been made extremely difficult, if not impossible, for important new competition to enter production or distribution. The present companies through contract agreements control the motion picture players and directors of established reputation, as well as other persons of high technical ability. Production personnel and production equipment may be jointly used through mutual loans. Facilities are not generally available to others on these terms.

The control of production and distribution by these companies is confirmed by their ownership of a most important segment of the motion picture theaters of the United States. A pretentious independent production in order to be profitable must be shown in at least some of these theaters, and in general this can be achieved only by entering into a distribution contract with one of the major companies. This fact makes it extremely difficult to finance any independent production unless such arrangements have already been made.

In their relationships with exhibitors these companies have demonstrated similarity in policy and action. Various practices have been developed to maintain their control over this field and to render it profitable. Where competition has proved counter to the joint interests of these companies, cooperation has been substituted. Many of the practices initiated and perpetuated by these companies must be considered definitely inimical to the interests of the consumer.

The motion picture industry is not unique in the sense that it is dominated by a few large companies. An even higher degree of concentration may be found in some other industries. But in many of these industries it can be demonstrated that combination has resulted in real economic benefits to the consumer. It is, therefore, pertinent to inquire what economic advantages have accrued to the consumer from the degree of concentration which exists in the production and distribution branches of the motion picture industry today.

A full and adequate discussion of this question would require information which is not available to the authors of this report. However, a few significant items may be considered. So far as production is concerned, the question to be answered is whether a larger number of producing units, each making a smaller number of pictures, would increase unit costs of production or lower the standard of film entertainment.

In this connection the experience of the United Artists Corporation is perhaps suggestive. The pictures distributed by this company almost uniformly meet a high standard of quality. Moreover, the number of pictures produced each year is not large. In the 1930 and 1931 seasons this company released 13 and 14 features, respectively; in the 1937 season the number was 16. Beyond this, it may be pointed out that most of the productions distributed by the United Artists Corporation are carried through by completely separate and individual producing organizations.

While this example is far from conclusive, since many important factors have been omitted from consideration, it nevertheless suggests that efficiency in production may perhaps be achieved on a much smaller number of pictures than the 40, 50, or 60 produced annually by each of the major companies.

It is not irrelevant in this connection to point out that Hollywood has been the target of repeated charges of extravagance and economic waste. It is unnecessary to detail these here. But inefficiency or extravagance of the type ordinarily alleged is seldom possible except in very large organizations. One must admit the possibility, then, that unit costs of production might actually be less if the producing companies were of smaller average size.

In the distribution branch of the industry, it must be admitted without question that there is a real cost advantage in having each distributor handle as large a number of pictures as possible. An increase in the number of distributing organizations would undoubtedly result in duplication of personnel and facilities. However, distribution costs are in general a rather small factor in this industry, and they do not increase in direct ratio as the number of prints released by each distributor is reduced.

Certain entries must be made on the other side of the ledger. The concentration existing in the production and distribution branches of the industry has permitted the concerted use of practices which insure a return from the consumer on all products, regardless of quality. The large business units existing are generally unresponsive to consumer pressure, and the economic forces tending to produce steady improvement of the goods offered have to some extent been vitiated.

For the production and distribution branches of the industry together, then, there is no strong evidence to show that the existing degree of concentration has resulted in economic savings for the consumer. The motion picture industry may be contrasted in this respect with the manufacture of automobiles. Here there is no question but that a high degree of integration exists. But it is equally true that this integration has been followed both by substantial and persistent reductions in unit costs of production and by steady improvements in quality.

Concentration is likewise an important factor in the exhibition branch of the industry. Individual theaters have been combined under common ownership and welded into huge chains of enormous pooled buying power. The economic strength of these chains has been used to enhance their profits and extend their sway at the expense of consumers and the smaller elements in the industry. Various practices have been developed and used when necessary to destroy the possibility of successful competition. Overbuying of films, unfair and unwarranted clearance and zoning agreements, and a variety of other practices have been actively employed in this way.

These practices represent more, however, than a simple abuse of the power conferred by size. They form a part of the larger problem of local monopoly in the exhibition field. Distributors of motion pictures frequently describe themselves as wholesalers. By inference exhibitors are to be likened to retailers. On closer examination, however, the parallel vanishes. Virtually any retail article sold at a nominal price may be marketed in a variety of retail outlets. Motion pictures, on the other hand, can be offered to the public only in motion picture theaters. Each theater represents a large investment and unlike the usual retail establishment it can be used only for a single specialized purpose.

Control of all theaters in a locality, therefore, gives the possessor the means of monopoly. A retail outlet of one type may in most cases be transformed almost overnight to an outlet for an entirely different commodity. An additional outlet for motion picture exhibition, on the other hand, cannot be found so readily. Control of all theaters in an area is as surely a monopoly as a local electric power or telephone company. Competition is absent simply because other facilities for the business are not available. The major difference is that the charges made by utilities are limited by public regulation.

It is assumed that whoever may wish to do so is free to construct a new theater. It may be said, therefore, that there can be no local monopoly of exhibition since inordinate profits would draw competition. Let us examine this prospect more closely.

It has already been pointed out that the construction of a new theater entails a considerable investment in property which will have but one use and which will be of little value if not put to that use. An investor would be foolish indeed if he did not examine the risks before embarking on such a prospect. It may be assumed, then, that the investor before constructing a new theater will insure that when it is completed an adequate supply of suitable pictures will be available for use. How frequently will this condition be satisfied in a locality where the control of existing theaters is in the hands of a large chain exhibition organization? Such organizations must feel secure indeed in their local monopolies since in general they have to fear competition only from organizations as powerful as themselves. Especially secure are the theater-operating subsidiaries of the major producer-distributors since every dictate of self-interest moves them to cooperate rather than compete with one another.

Here again one may inquire whether real economies to the consumer may not result from chain operation. The most significant answer to this question is given by the fact that acquisition of a theater by a chain is seldom followed by a reduction in the charged admission price. Rather, the reverse has more commonly been the case. The spread of chain exhibition organizations has accomplished a steady increase in the number of local exhibition monopolies, the effect of which has been gradually to strip the consumer of the protection formerly accorded him by competition.

Concentration in both production and exhibition has been linked through the five major companies which operate in both branches of the industry. The activities of these companies in each of these fields have been used to extend their control and enhance their profits in the other. In the exhibition as well as in the production field, cooperation has been substituted for competition where this was jointly advantageous, without consideration of the interests of the consumer. The theater interests of these companies have been so located as to ·

provide a minimum degree of friction of one with the other. Conflicting interests have been resolved where this seemed mutually desirable by simply pooling theater operations.

It has been stated that the degree of concentration existing in the motion picture industry is not greater and in some cases is less than that obtaining in many other important lines of enterprise. It may be asked, then, why this industry requires any special consideration. One answer to this question has been given above. In some lines of enterprise, concentration confers cost advantages which in turn benefit the consumer. In the motion picture industry, on the other hand, there is reason to believe that exactly the opposite has been the case. In at least one other important aspect the motion picture industry displays significant differences.

The motion picture commenced as a novel and pleasing type of entertainment, but it has evolved into an important social and cultural force. In some senses it provides a common denominator to the feelings and aspirations of an entire people. Its importance must then be measured in terms other than the conventional one of dollars and cents.

Readers of economic reports of this type have come to expect a diagnosis of sickness, to be followed by the author's pet patent medicine for the cure of all troubles. In the present case the authors are content to indicate the cause without attempting to make a sale on some particular cure. However, one thing may be definitely stated. Any remedy or solution to the problems of the motion picture industry in its relations with the consuming public will not be a simple one. It is a mistake to assume that any such cure-all as "divorcement of exhibition from production" or "restoration of competition in the production field" or any other single proposal will resolve all the difficulties of all the elements with an interest in this industry. Any single step might well ameliorate the effects of some of the undesirable practices of the industry as they affect the consumer, the exhibitor or some other interested group. The motion picture industry exhibits symptoms which are common to many of our great enterprises. Its problems are part of the larger problem of the development and direction of American industry. More than anything else, perhaps, intelligent and sympathetic study is indicated.

APPENDIX I

THE EIGHT MAJOR COMPANIES

APPENDIX I

THE EIGHT MAJOR COMPANIES

The following are brief sketches of the development and integration of the five major producer-distributor-exhibitor companies and the three satellite producer-distributor companies.

The extent of the financial holdings of these companies is of necessity understated. For instance, interests in real estate, radio, and music companies among others are not included.

The material in the sketches is taken from the amended and supplemental complaint, November 14, 1940, *U. S.* v. *Paramount Pictures, et al.*, civil action No. 87,273, in the District Court of the United States for the Southern District of New York.

PARAMOUNT PICTURES, INC.

Famous Players-Lasky Corporation was incorporated on July 19, 1916. In 1917 twelve producing companies merged with it. At the same time the corporation integrated production and distribution by acquiring a national distribution system through a merger with Artcraft Pictures Corporation and Paramount Pictures Corporation.

In 1919 the corporation started its theater acquisition program. It acquired stock interest in Southern Enterprises, Inc., with 135 theaters in the South; in 1920 it acquired stock interest in New England Theatres, Inc., with 50 New England theaters; in the Butterfield Theatre Circuit with 70 theaters in Michigan about 1926; in Balaban & Katz with 50 theaters in Illinois at the same time. Later numerous theaters in the West and Middle West were acquired.

In April 1927 the corporate name was changed to Paramount Famous Lasky Corporation, and in April 1930 to Paramount Publix Corporation. In 1933 Paramount Publix Corporation was adjudicated a bankrupt in the Federal District Court for the Southern District of New York. In June 1935 it was reorganized under sec. 77B of the Bankruptcy Act under the name of Paramount Pictures, Inc.

Today Paramount operates 63 first-run metropolitan and 1,210 other theaters, and has exchanges in 33 key cities. It produces from 45 to 60 pictures annually and ordinarily distributes each season a substantial number of features produced by others for release by it; it produces an average of 45 short subjects and 104 news reels annually.

Its gross assets are approximately $90,000,000, and for the fiscal year ended in 1939 its consolidated gross income was in excess of $100,000,000.

LOEW'S INCORPORATED

Loew's Consolidated Enterprises, organized in 1910 was succeeded in 1911 by Loew's Theatrical Enterprises. Beginning in 1911 the company, through subsidiary corporations, extended its activities in the operation of theaters in New York City, among other cities. By 1919 it had financial interests in approximately 56 theaters.

In October 1919 Loew's Incorporated was organized and acquired all the outstanding stock of Loew's Theatrical Enterprises. The extent of its theater business has increased gradually since.

In 1920 Loew's Inc., entered the production and distribution field by acquiring the outstanding stock of Metro Pictures Corporation. In 1924 Metro merged with Goldwyn Pictures Corporation under the name of Metro-Goldwyn Pictures Corporation. As a result of the merger Loew's became the owner of all of Metro-Goldwyn's common stock. About the same time certain assets of Louis B. Mayer Pictures, Inc., were turned over to Metro-Goldwyn. The business of Metro-Goldwyn was subsequently assumed by the Metro-Goldwyn-Mayer Corporation. In December 1937, the Metro-Goldwyn-Mayer Corporation ceased to do business and its production activities were taken over by Loew's Incorporated.

Today Loew's operates 24 first-run metropolitan and 98 other theaters and has exchanges in 31 key cities. It produces from 40 to 50 pictures annually and ordinarily distributes each season a substantial number of features produced by others for release by it; it produces an average of 36 shorts annually.

Its gross assets are approximately $150,000,000, and for the fiscal year ended in 1939 its consolidated gross income was in excess of $100,000,000.

TWENTIETH CENTURY-FOX FILM CORPORATION

On February 1, 1915, this organization was incorporated under the name of Fox Film Corporation. In August 1925 it acquired about one-third the common stock of West Coast Theatres, Inc., with theaters in California and other Western States. In March 1928 it purchased all the common stock of Wesco Corporation, a holding company for theater operation.

In 1933 Wesco went into receivership, but in 1934 readjusted its capital structure, and the Chase National Bank of the City of New York acquired 58 percent of its stock, the Fox Film Corporation retaining 42 percent.

In August 1935 the Chase Bank acquired a substantial stock interest in Twentieth-Century Pictures, Inc., a producing and distributing company, and the name was changed to Twentieth Century-Fox Film Corporation. The name of Wesco was changed to National Theatres Corporation.

In 1937 the corporation acquired all the common stock of Roxy Theatre, Inc., which owns Roxy in New York.

Today Twentieth Century-Fox operates 30 first-run metropolitan and 508 other theaters; it has exchanges in 31 key cities. It produces annually from 50 to 60 pictures and distributes a substantial number of features produced by others for release by it; it produces an average of 20 short subjects and 104 news reels annually.

Its gross assets are approximately $60,000,000, and for the fiscal year ended in 1939 its consolidated gross income was about $50,000,000.

WARNER BROTHERS PICTURES, INC.

Warner Bros. was incorporated in 1923 for the purpose of producing, distributing, and exhibiting motion pictures. At the time it had no theaters, but in December 1924 it entered the exhibition field with one theater in Youngstown, Ohio. In 1925 it acquired Vitagraph, Inc., which operated 34 exchanges in the principal cities of this country and Canada; it also acquired two other affiliated companies operating foreign exchanges.

In 1925 it acquired 13 additional theaters and in December 1928 it acquired the majority stock of Stanley Co. of America with 182 theaters and partial stock in other theater companies which owned or leased 51 theaters in the Middle Atlantic States and District of Columbia. Subsequently it acquired theater interests in 11 other States.

Warner Bros. operates 35 first-run metropolitan and 522 other theaters; it has exchanges in 34 cities in this country and Canada. It produces more than 50 features each season and ordinarily distributes some features each season produced by others for release by it.

Its gross assets are approximately $150,000,000, and for the fiscal year ended in 1939 its consolidated gross income exceeded $100,000,000.

RADIO-KEITH-ORPHEUM CORPORATION

The Keith-Albee-Orpheum Corporation was organized January 28, 1928. In February 1928 it acquired all the outstanding stock of the B. F. Keith Corporation, with a large number, of theaters in the East, and approximately 90 percent of the outstanding stock of the Orpheum Circuit, Inc., with theaters in the Midwest and West. It incorporated October 25, 1928, as Radio-Keith-Orpheum Corporation, after securing control of Keith-Albee-Orpheum and the controlling interest in other companies engaged in exhibition, the most important ones being R-K-O Proctor Corporation (a New York circuit) and R-K-O Midwest Corporation (Ohio and Michigan theaters).

F-B-O Productions, Inc., the principal producing company taken over by R-K-O, was later renamed R-K-O Radio Pictures, Inc. In January 1931, it took over the news reel and other production facilities of Pathé Exchange, Inc., and later those of the Van Buren Corporation.

On January 27, 1933, the R-K-O Corporation went into an equity receivership, and the Irving Trust Co. was appointed receiver. On June 8, 1934, R-K-O Corporation filed a petition for reorganization under section 77B of the Bankruptcy Act in the District Court for the Southern District of New York. The Irving Trust Co. was appointed trustee in reorganization. A plan of reorganization was approved January 17, 1939, confirmed April 11, 1939, and affirmed by the Circuirt Court of Appeals for the Second Circuit on September 8, 1939.

Today R-K-O operates 29 first-run metropolitan and 103 other theaters; it has exchanges in 32 cities. It produces over 40 pictures annually and ordinarily distributes a substantial number of features produced by others for release by it; it produces an average of 91 shorts and 104 news reels annually.

Its gross assets are approximately $70,000,000, and for the fiscal year ended in 1939 its consolidated gross income was about $40,000,000.

UNITED ARTISTS CORPORATION

United Artists was organized in 1919 by a group of producers for the purpose of distributing the features produced by its organizers. The corporation is owned by four stockholders: Samuel Goldwyn, Mary Pickford, the estate of Douglas Fairbanks, and Alexander Korda.

It releases not quite 20 pictures yearly and maintains exchanges in 26 cities.

It issues no public statement of gross assets or business done. For the fiscal year ended in 1939 its consolidated gross income was over $10,000,000.

COLUMBIA PICTURES CORPORATION

Columbia was incorporated January 10, 1924. Early the following year it acquired the assets of C. B. C. Film Sales Corporation, and continued buying up various exchanges throughout the country. In 1928 it acquired, through merger, Screen Snapshots, Inc., Hall Room Boys Photoplays, Inc., Starland Revue, Inc.—all short subjects producing companies. By 1929 its distribution system was organized on a national scale, and in 1930 it secured exchanges in foreign countries. In 1931 it secured 50 percent of the capital stock of Screen Gems, Inc., producer of shorts, and in 1937 secured the remaining 50 percent.

Today it produces from 35 to 55 features annually and ordinarily distributes a substantial number of features produced by others for release by it. It produces an average of 61 short subjects annually. It operates 32 exchanges in key cities.

Its gross assets are approximately $15,000,000, and for the fiscal year ended in 1939 its consolidated gross income was about $20,000,000.

UNIVERSAL CORPORATION

Universal Pictures Corporation, formerly Universal Film Manufacturing Co., was incorporated in New York in 1912. On January 10, 1925, Universal Pictures Co., Inc., was formed and about the same time purchased the entire outstanding capital stock of Universal Pictures Corporation.

In January 1926 Universal Pictures Corporation secured substantial stock interest in Universal Chain Theatres Corporation—exhibitors. In 1928 this exhibition corporation and its affiliates operated 315 theaters in Canada, the District of Columbia, and 20 States, including the Griffith Amusement Co., with 40 theaters in Oklahoma and Texas, and the Schine chain, with 90 theaters in New York and Ohio. Between 1929 and 1931 it disposed of a substantial number of theaters. In 1933 it went into receivership and the remaining theaters were sold by the receiver.

From 1925 to 1936 Universal Pictures Corporation was the production branch of Universal Pictures Co., Inc. In December 1936 Universal Pictures Corporation was dissolved and its assets were transferred to Universal Pictures Co., Inc. Universal Corporation, organized in April 1936, acquired the controlling stock interest of Universal Pictures Co., Inc. (producer), and the Big U Film exchange (distributor).

Today Universal produces 40 to 45 pictures annually and ordinarily distributes each season some features produced by others for release by it. It distributes extensively through the Big U Film Exchange, Inc., and Universal Film Exchanges, Inc.

Its gross assets are approximately $12,000,000, and for the fiscal year ended in 1939 its consolidated gross income was about $20,000,000.

APPENDIX II

THE MOTION PICTURE PRODUCERS AND DISTRIBUTORS OF AMERICA, INC.

OR

THE HAYS ORGANIZATION

APPENDIX II

THE MOTION PICTURE PRODUCERS AND DISTRIBUTORS OF AMERICA, INC., OR THE HAYS ORGANIZATION

Early in the 1920's there was great public disapproval of a wave of salacious films. Aggravated by a series of scandals involving motion-picture personalities, this indignation resulted in widespread public agitation for censorship of motion pictures both locally and by the Federal Government. Considering censorship undesirable in itself and fearing such action might be the first step to further governmental control, the industry attempted to put its own house in order. Thus in 1922 it formed the Motion Picture Producers & Distributors of America, Inc. Perhaps not solely because of his abilities as an administrator, the industry hired to head this organization a prominent political figure, Will H. Hays, then Postmaster General and chairman of the Republican National Committee.

This organization successfully combated the censorship drive of the period, primarily by voluntary restraint in production. However, the many pictures narrowly skirting the borderline of decency which have been released since then very clearly illustrate that the interest of the organization was not in cleaning up motion pictures from a pure moral standpoint; rather, it was to keep motion picture entertainment at a level which would not so far violate the mores of the time that renewed censorship activities would come into play.

A gradual disregard of pledges following the initial clean-up finally led to the formation of the Legion of Decency early in 1934 as a religious crusade against immoral films. This was followed on July 1, 1934, by a new and more stringent Production Code of Ethics which successfully resisted the renewed attempt to write censorship clauses into the law. It was directed by Joseph I. Breen, whose findings were "subject to review only on appeal to the company presidents of member companies in New York."[1]

Although the Hays organization was created primarily in answer to the threat of censorship, it quite naturally extended its field to resist other activities which might lead to control over the industry by Government. Today it is a regular function of the Hays organization to represent the larger companies before State and Federal legislative bodies. Nor have the activities of the organization been limited to this simple field. The interests of the organization have spread through a number of activities which the large companies felt could be profitably and legally entered into on a cooperative basis. The following paragraphs briefly outline some of these activities.

---

[1] 1935-36 Motion Picture Almanac, p. 800.

PRODUCTION CODE ADMINISTRATION

The Production Code consists of a rather detailed statement of undesirable scenes or situations or methods of production which the members of the Hays organization have pledged themselves to avoid. Since a simple pledge of this kind is more likely to be honored in the breach rather than the observance, a Production Code Administration has been formed to implement it. The Production Code Administration reviews all completed films submitted by members or nonmembers. It will review scripts, but does not give prior approval merely from the reading of a script.

Objectionable material in a photoplay must be removed before the Hays office places it seal of approval on the film. The code has definite teeth, in that the members of the Hays organization have agreed to pay a $25,000 fine to the organization for the exhibition in any affiliated theater of any picture which lacks the seal of approval.

It is evident that refusal of the seal of approval to a first-class independent production would immediately make it a financial failure because it could not be shown in any of the 2,800 theaters controlled by the large companies. It might not even be necessary flatly to refuse the seal of approval. Granting the seal might be made conditional on the deletion of small parts of the film which nevertheless served to destroy the essential appeal of the picture.

It is true that few complaints have been made by independent producers regarding the activities of the Production Code Administration. But, even granting that the powers of the code administration have in every case been wisely and equitably used, there remains a definite question as to whether such control of the business of potential or prospective competitors can properly be lodged in the hands of an interested industry group. The motion picture industry has over the years consistently opposed governmental censorship of films largely on the grounds that the power of censorship might not be wisely exercised. How much more assurance is there that this power will always be wisely exercised by a nongovernmetal group?

ADVERTISING ADVISORY COUNCIL

This council, organized in 1933, performs the same functions with respect to motion picture advertising as the Production Code Administration exercises with respect to a photoplay's content. Members of the Hays organization are required to use advertising approved by the council exclusively. Nonobservance is punishable by a fine of from $1,000 to $5,000. The implications of the control of advertising are perhaps less serious than the censorship activities, since these do not appear to limit to the same extent the activities of persons outside the association.

TITLE REGISTRATION BUREAU

This bureau was set up for the purpose of registering motion picture titles to avoid the unintentional use of similar or identical titles.

THEATER SERVICE DEPARTMENT

This is an affiliated exhibitors relations department. Among its activities it assists "trade associations of theater owners in developing in constructive ways their own usefulness and service to the local theater owners in their own state and zone   *   *   *" [2]

FOREIGN DEPARTMENT

Through this department, "the Association assists members in securing fair treatment in the distribution of American films abroad. In the 17 years, the Association has taken a leading part in successful negotiations to solve difficulties due to restrictive legislation. The department keeps member companies closely informed on legislative and economic developments in foreign markets." [3]

MISCELLANEOUS

Among the other activities are the Conservation Department, whose function it is to eliminate fire hazards in film exchanges; the Community Service Department, whose function it is to stimulate public interest in and patronage of films of the higher type; the general Counsel, who represents the organization before the legislative bodies; the Legal Department, which is adviser to the Association and its members; the Public Information Department, the Treasury and Accounting Department; and the Office of the President.

COPYRIGHT BUREAU

The function of this bureau is to ferret out violations of copyrights. It is contended to be separate from the Hays organization, but is financed by the same companies.

FILM BOARDS OF TRADE

These boards of trade were established in various key cities by and for the producers and distributors.

The film boards of trade undertook to settle disputes between exhibitors and chains of producers. Attached to each film board of trade was a credit committee. If a credit committee reported adversely to an exhibitor, all of the member producers and distributors withdrew their product from the affected theater. *The United States* v. *First National Pictures et al.* (282 U. S. 44) decreed that certain acts of the credit committee constituted an illegal restraint of trade.[4]

It is denied by the Hays organization that there is any connection between it and the film boards of trade, but they are financed by the same organizations and both groups have the same general counsel and general attorney.[5]

ASSOCIATION OF MOTION PICTURE PRODUCERS OF CALIFORNIA, INC.

This is an association of the California producers. Its composition is similar to that of the Hays organization. It operates the Central Casting Bureau, which supplies the members of the association with

---

[1] "Film Facts," published by the Motion Picture Producers and Distributors of America, New York, 1940.
[2] Ibid.
[4] Cit. from hearings before a subcommittee of the Committee on Interstate Commerce, U. S. Senate, pursuant to S. 3012, "Compulsory Block-Booking and Blind Selling in the Motion Picture Industry," 74th Cong., Feb. 27 and 28, 1936, p. 16.
[5] Ibid.

actors above extra grade, and the Call Bureau which supplies members with extra players. These services are not supplied to nonmembers.

OFFICERS, DIRECTORS, AND MEMBERS OF THE MOTION PICTURE PRODUCERS AND DISTRIBUTORS OF AMERICA, INC.[6]

OFFICERS

President_____ Will H. Hays.
Secretary_____ Carl E. Milliken.
Treasurer_____ Frederick L. Herron.
Assistant treasurer and assistant secretary_____ George Borthwick.

DIRECTORS

WILL H. HAYS, *Chairman*

Barney Balaban, Paramount.
Nate J. Blumberg, Universal.
Jack Cohn, Columbia.
Cecil B. de Mille, producer.
E. W. Hammons, Education Pictures.
E. B. Hatrick, News of the Day.
Frederick L. Herron.
Walter Wanger, United Artists.

S. R. Kent, Twentieth Century Fox.
Sol Lesser, producer and exhibitor.
Hal E. Roach, United Artists.
G. J. Schaefer, United Artists.
N. M. Schenck, Loew's.
Maurice Silverstone.
Maj. A. Warner, Vitaphone Corporation.
Harry M. Warner, Warner Bros.

MEMBERS

Bray Productions, Inc.
The Caddo Co., Inc.
Columbia Pictures Corporation.
Cosmopolitan Corporation.
Cecil B. de Mille Productions, Inc.
Walt Disney Productions, Ltd.
Eastman Kodak Co.
Educational Films Corporation of America.
Electrical Research Products, Inc.
First National Pictures, Inc.
Samuel Goldwyn, Inc.
D. W. Griffith, Inc.
Inspiration Pictures, Inc.
Loew's, Inc.
Paramount Pictures, Inc.

Pioneer Pictures, Inc.
Principal Pictures Corporation.
RCA Manufacturing Co., Inc.
R-K-O Radio Pictures, Inc.
Reliance Pictures, Inc.
Hal Roach Studios, Inc.
Selznick International Pictures, Inc.
Terrytoons, Inc.
Twentieth Century-Fox Film Corporation.
United Artists Corporation.
Universal Pictures Co., Inc.
Vitagraph, Inc.
Walter Wanger Productions, Inc.
Warner Bros. Pictures, Inc.

OFFICERS, DIRECTORS, AND MEMBERS OF THE ASSOCIATION OF MOTION PICTURE PRODUCERS OF CALIFORNIA, INC.[6]

OFFICERS

President_____ Y. Frank Freeman, vice-president, Paramount.
First Vice-President_____ Edgar J. Mannix, producer at M-G-M.
Second Vice-President_____ Cliff Work, executive, R-K-O.
Executive Vice-President and Secretary-Treasurer.   Fred W. Beetson.

DIRECTORS

Harry Cohn_____ President, Columbia.
Y. Frank Freeman_____ Vice president, Paramount.
Samuel Goldwyn_____ Producer and executive United Artists.
Edgar J. Mannix_____ Producer at M-G-M.
J. R. McDonough_____ Vice president, R-K-O.

[6] " m Facts," published by the Motion Picture Producers and Distributors of America, New York, 1940. Fil

Hal E. Roach_____ Producer, member United Artists.
James Roosevelt_____ .
Joseph M. Schenck_____ Executive, Twentieth Century-
Fox.
Walter F. Wanger_____ Producer, member United Artists.
J. L. Warner_____ Executive, Warner Bros., First
National Studios.
Cliff Work_____ Executive, R-K-O.

MEMBERS

Columbia Pictures Corporation.
Globe Productions, Inc.
Samuel Goldwyn, Inc., Ltd.
Loew's, Incorporated.
Paramount Pictures, Inc.
RKO-Radio Pictures, Inc.

Hal E. Roach Studios, Inc.
Twentieth Century-Fox Film Corporation.
Universal Pictures Company, Inc.
Walter Wanger Productions, Inc.
Warner Brothers Pictures, Inc.

APPENDIX III

THE CONSENT DECREE

APPENDIX III

THE CONSENT DECREE

"And the return of an industry to the competitive design is so rare a product of litigation. * * *" [1]

After years of charges and counter charges of unfair trade practices by members of the motion picture industry and the theater-going public, the Department of Justice on July 20, 1938, filed a petition in equity [2] against the five major producer-distributor-exhibitor companies (Paramount, Loew's, Radio-Keith-Orpheum, Warner Bros., and Twentieth Century-Fox) and the three large producer-distributors (United Artists, Columbia, and Universal) charging them with combining and conspiring to retrain trade and commerce in the production, distribution, and exhibition of motion pictures in the United States, and with attempting successfully to monopolize such trade and commerce in violation of the Sherman Act. In this petition and in its amended and supplemental complaint of November 14, 1940, the Department of Justice listed the various ways by which it allege these purposes were accomplished.

The following were among the offenses charged against the eight companies:

Mutual loaning of production personnel and equipment without extending these privileges to independent producers on the same terms.

Fixing of license terms in contracts before licensees have the opportunity to estimate the value and character of films and before trade showing or completion of films.

Fixing of run, clearance, and minimum admission price terms.

Conditioning the licensing of one group of films on that of another.

Conditioning the licensing of films in one theater upon licensing in other theaters under common ownership or control.

Discrimination with respect to license terms granted to theaters in large circuits because they are part of a circuit.

In discriminating between circuits and independent theaters, it is alleged that these companies—

Make exclusive contracts with circuit theaters in some localities.

Withhold prints to give circuit theaters clearance not agreed to in contracts.

Permit negotiation of unfair clearance by circuits.

Set minimum admission prices of independent exhibitors so that they cannot successfully compete with circuit theaters.

Prohibit independent exhibitors from playing on a double-feature program a picture previously played by a circuit theater.

Grant selective contracts to circuit theaters but not to independents.

Designate play dates.

Force short subjects and newsreels on independent theaters.

Charge independent theaters higher film rentals than circuits in equivalent situations.

Partially defray advertising costs of circuit theaters, but not those of independents.

Require that independent theaters, but not circuit theaters, pay score charges.

---

[1] Temporary National Economic Committee, Monograph 16, "Antitrust in Action," Walton Hamilton and Irene Till, 1940, p. 57.
[2] *United States* v. *Paramount Pictures, Inc., et al.*, op. cit.

Permit circuit theaters to modify contract terms with respect to film rentals, transfer of pictures from one theater to another, cancelation of some pictures to permit extended run on more successful features, and the like, without extending similar privileges to independent exhibitors.

The following additional charges were made against the five producer-distributor-exhibitor companies:

Conditioning licensing of films distributed by one in the theaters of the other on the licensing of films of the other in the theaters of the former.

Excluding independent productions from affiliated theaters.

Excluding independent exhibitors from operating first-run theaters where affiliated theaters are located.

Excluding independent exhibitors from the same subsequent-run as affiliated theaters in cities where both are located.

Using affiliated theaters to control film supply, run, clearance, and admission prices.

Coercing and intimidating independent exhibitors into licensing films on arbitrary terms by threatening to build or acquire competing theater.

Coercing and intimidating independent exhibitors into relinquishing part or whole interest in a theater to one of the affiliated companies by threatening to build or acquire competing theaters.

Eliminating competition by jointly operating theaters.

Dividing available films between two or more affiliated theaters in the same competitive area, thus eliminating competition.

Refraining from competition with each other in the exhibition field.

To end these conditions, the Department of Justice asked of the court:

* * * That each of the contracts, combinations, and conspiracies in restraint of interstate trade and commerce, together with the attempts to monopolize and the monopolization of the same, hereinbefore described, be declared illegal and violative of the Sherman Act.

* * * That the defendants herein, their subsidiaries * * * be perpetually enjoined and restrained from continuing to carry out, directly or indirectly, expressly or impliedly, the attempts at monopolization, the monopolies and all restraints of said interstate trade and commerce in the production, distribution, and exhibition of motion pictures described herein, and from entering into and carrying out, directly or indirectly, expressly or impliedly, any monopolies or restraints of interstate trade and commerce similar to those alleged herein to be illegal.

* * * That a nation-wide system of impartial arbitration tribunals or such other means of enforcement as the court may deem proper be established pursuant to the final decree of this court in order to secure adequate enforcement of whatever general and nation-wide prohibitions of illegal practices may be contained therein.

* * * That the integration of the production and exhibition branches of the industry by the producer-exhibitor defendants herein, and each of them, be declared to be unlawful as an instrumentality of monopoly and restraint upon interstate trade and commerce, and violative of the Sherman Anti-Trust Act.

* * * That the defendants Paramount Pictures, Inc., Twentieth Century-Fox Film Corporation, Warner Bros. Pictures, Inc., Loew's, Inc., and Radio-Keith-Orpheum Corporation, and each of them, under the direction and supervision of the court be ordered and directed to divest themselves of all interest and ownership, both direct and indirect, either in theaters and theater holdings or in production and distribution facilities and that they, and each of them * * * be permanently enjoined from acquiring, directly or indirectly, any other interests in the branch of the industry divested or in any persons, firms, or corporations which are engaged or may engage in that branch of the industry; said divestiture to be accomplished and carried out upon such terms and conditions as the court may deem proper.

* * * That the defendants Paramount Pictures, Inc., Twentieth Century-Fox Film Corporation, National Theatre Corporation, Warner Bros. Pictures, Inc., Warner Bros. Circuit Management Corporation, Loew's, Inc., Radio-Keith-Orpheum Corporation, Keith-Albee-Orpheum Corporation, R. K. O. Proctor Corporation, and R-K-O Midwest Corporation and each of them * * * be ordered and directed to divest themselves of all interests and ownership, both direct and indirect, in any theaters which the court shall find have been used by one or more of them to unreasonably restrain trade and commerce in motion

pictures in violation of section 1 of the Sherman Act or to monopolize trade and commerce in motion pictures in violation of section 2 of the Sherman Act. * * *

The parties to the suit went through the usual preliminary maneuvers appropriate to such a situation. The actual trial, originally scheduled to begin early in 1940, was postponed several times. Finally, on October 29, the Department of Justice announced that the five major producer-distributor-exhibitor companies had agreed to a consent decree. The decree, entered by the court on November 20, 1940, ended the suit for the five affiliated companies, but continued it for the three producer-distributor companies who refused to assent to it.

With respect to the demand of the Department of Justice that exhibition and production be separated (see the last three of the paragraphs quoted above from the complaint) the consent decree provided in section XXI:

Petitioner, by its counsel, has represented to the Court that the public interest requires that the provisions of this decree shall operate for a trial period of three years from the date of entry hereof. Petitioner has further represented to the Court, and each of the consenting defendants has consented to the entry of this decree upon the condition, that Petitioner will not for a period of three years after the entry of this decree, either in this action or any other action or proceeding against any such defendant seek either the relief or any thereof prayed in * * * the Petition filed herein July 20, 1938, or in * * * the Amended and Supplemental Complaint filed herein November 14, 1940, or otherwise seek to divorce the production or distribution of motion pictures from their exhibition; or to dissolve any such defendant or any corporation in which any such defendant has, directly or indirectly, a substantial stock interest and which is engaged in the exhibition of motion pictures or holds directly or indirectly a substantial stock interest in any corporation so engaged, or to dissolve or break up any circuit of theaters of any such defendant or of any such corporation, or to require any such defendant, corporation or circuit to divest itself of its interests or any thereof, direct or indirect, in motion-picture theaters in which it had an interest at the date of the entry of this decree.

This particular demand, then, that exhibition and production be separated, was thus withdrawn.

The decree embodies a number of agreements intended to modify or eliminate the undesirable features of certain industry practices. With respect to block booking, the consenting distributors agree that after August 31, 1941, they will sell films in blocks of not more than five pictures each, and will make sale of each block in no way contingent on the sale of any other block. To eliminate blind selling, it is agreed that after the same date all pictures will be previewed in each exchange area prior to sale. The distributors further agree: To cease forcing shorts, reissues, westerns, newsreels, and the like; to consider only the theaters in each exchange area in contract negotiations with a circuit; to submit to arbitration any questions of unfair clearance; to permit cancelation of features for cause; and to cease acquiring new theaters as part of any general program of theater acquisition.

The decree also contains several escape clauses. These have special reference to the agreements to sell in blocks of not more than five pictures and to trade show all features. The most important of these stipulates that, if prior to June 1, 1942, restrictions at least as stringent have not been placed on the activities of the three producer-distributors not consenting to the decree, these provisions shall become inoperative after September 1, 1942, with respect to the consenting defendants.

On November 14, 1940, before the consent decree was entered, a formal hearing on it was held by the court. At this time, other persons interested in the outcome of the Government's suit were permitted to express their opinions. Representatives of virtually every important exhibitor association in the industry and of the three non-consehting defendants expressed opposition to the decree. The opposition was so unanimous that one of the Government's attorneys said: "The court seems to have more friends than the decree." [3]

Soon after this, the Motion Picture Research Council and various groups interested in improving the moral standards of motion picture entertainment also condemned the decree.

The press release in which the Department of Justice originally announced the filing of an antitrust suit against the major motion picture companies stated:

Suit may develop need for congressional action.—Until the evidence is produced, it is too early to state whether the antitrust laws by themselves are sufficiently effective to restore competitive conditions. If it appears from such evidence that further aid is needed, the results of the investigation and trial will be brought to the attention of Congress.

The Department desires that this suit result in the clarification of the antitrust laws with respect to the motion picture industry.

The application of the general principles of the antitrust laws to particular industries demands distinctions which cannot be drawn in advance of the production of actual proof. They can only be staked out with respect to particular industries through the clarifying process of judicial action. This is the purpose of this suit.[4]

Nevertheless, section I of the consent decree reads in part as follows:

The Petitioner not having offered any proof of its allegations that defendants have violated the antitrust laws, and defendants having denied each and every such allegation, this Court has not determined or adjudicated and by this decree does not determine or adjudicate, and this is not a decree to the effect that any of said defendants has violated or is now violating any of such laws, or any other statute; and this decree relates solely to future conduct herein below specified and is not based upon any finding, determination, or adjudication that any right or statute has yet been or is now being violated.

The entrance of the consent decree thus insures that any proof which the Department of Justice may have had of evidence of violation of the antitrust laws by the five major companies will not be presented to the court and will not become available to the general public or to the Congress. Moreover, any evidence which might indicate that the problems of the industry cannot be met within the existing framework of the antitrust laws is likewise not disclosed. The efforts of the Department of Justice in gathering and sifting information over a period of years are thus nullified. Neither the Congress nor other interested parties are able to draw on this experience in order to appraise: (*a*) The extent or validity of complaints of combination in the industry; (*b*) the extent to which a consent decree will correct these conditions; (*c*) the extent to which additional or different remedies are necessary to restore a healthier competitive situation.

A further aspect of the consent decree may be indicated. The provisions of the decree with respect to trade showing and block booking represent a major concession on the part of the five affiliated companies. As stated, however, these provisions are to become inoperative after August 31, 1942, unless prior to that time conditions at least as restrictive have been either consented to or imposed by the court on the three satellite producing companies—Columbia, Universal, and United Artists. The continuation of these concessions is thus in

[3] "Variety," November 20, 1940.
[4] Release, Department of Justice, July 20, 1938.

no small part contingent on the strength of the Government's case against these three companies. None of these companies owns or operates theaters. Each is smaller than any of the five affiliated companies. It is obvious that many of the complaints of unfair practices which might be made and proved with respect to the five affiliated companies are in no way applicable to these three.

The Government's case against these three companies is, therefore, necessarily very much weaker than it is against any one of the other five producer-distributor-exhibitors. In one sense then, the major companies, by making certain concessions, have been able to negotiate a suspension of the Government's suit for a period of at least 3 years, while at the same time the extent of these concessions is limited by the success of the Government in prosecuting a much weaker case.

Finally, it has been shown in the body of this report that the misuse of economic power attained by linking together numerous separate operating units into large and powerful organizations has been responsible for many of those features and practices of the industry which are undesirable from the consumers' standpoint. It is relevant to point out, then, that the decree does not create any new competing units; rather, it freezes the present competitive situation. As a matter of fact, one of the escape clauses is designed to relieve the consenting companies from certain of the restrictions of the decree should any marked change in present relationships occur.

The remaining pages of this appendix are devoted to a brief analysis of the relation of various provisions of the decree to certain industry practices.

 *   *   *   *   ⁻

BLOCK BOOKING AND BLIND SELLING

With respect to blind selling, section III of the consent decree provides:

No consenting defendant engaged in the distribution of motion pictures * * * shall license or offer for license a feature motion picture * * * for public exhibition within the United States of America at which an admission fee is to be charged, until the feature has been trade shown within the exchange district in which the public exhibition is to be held.

The purpose of this section is to enable exhibitors and interested public welfare groups to learn about pictures before contracts for them are made.

The decree's answer to the problems raised by block booking is contained in section IV (a), which provides:

No distributor defendant shall offer for license or shall license more than five features in a single group. In offering its features for license to an exhibitor a distributor may change the combinations of features in groups as it may from time to time determine, and may license or offer for license as many groups of features as it may from time to time determine, provided that the license or offer for license of one group of features shall not be conditioned upon the licensing of another feature or group of features.

This provision does not eliminate block booking. It merely limits the size of blocks to 5 or less rather than 40 or 50 features.

It will be noted that the distributor is specifically left free to determine which features shall be grouped to form these blocks, and that he is not required to offer blocks of identical composition to different or competing theaters. Each exhibitor, of course, is free to negotiate for such combinations of pictures as he may desire out of all those released by a distributor. At the same time, it may be assumed that the distributor will try to use a good picture of proved box-office merit to "carry" four others that lack sufficient appeal to sell themselves.

Moreover, it is probable that even such cancelation privileges as the exhibitor previously received will be eliminated by this method of selling. It is true that section VII of the decree provides machinery for cancelation of certain pictures, but only on the grounds that they are generally offensive on moral, racial, or religious grounds in the particular localities in which the theaters are located, and only then after an arbitration hearing, if this is requested by the distributor.

There is thus a real question as to whether the ability of the exhibitor to select exactly those pictures he desires will be materially improved by this method of marketing. It is because of this that the decree has been uniformly opposed by the groups interested in improving the moral standards of film entertainment.

The provision has another feature which exhibitors consider undesirable. It will be remembered that continuity of film supply is an important factor to each exhibitor, and that the exhibitor generally does not oppose block booking as such but only its compulsory aspects. This provision, exhibitors fear, will jeopardize the continuous flow of product on which stable operation depends. The independent exhibitor associations which appeared before the Court before the decree was entered attacked the blocks-of-five provision principally for this reason, and stated that an unrestricted 20 percent cancelation privilege would be far more useful to them.

The exact effect which this method of sale will have on film prices is uncertain. Films will now be sold not only in the fall when attendance is high, but also during the box-office doldrums in the summer and in Lent. Also, the distributor will be impelled to make contracts promptly after previewing, since the price of features tends to decline with time. Moreover, with greater control of their playing time exhibitors may feel more free to fill in with occasional satisfactory independent productions. By shrewd trading exhibitors may be able to improve their position. On the other hand, the distributor may use uncertainty regarding future film supply to drive a hard bargain with the exhibitor. It is also quite probable that this method of selling will to some extent increase sales expense and that this will be reflected in higher prices.

There is one definite result. The independent exhibitor has complained that because of having to purchase the full output of several distributors, he occasionally has been required to license more features during the year than actually needed to operate his theater. Under the present system the exhibitor cannot be confronted at the end of the season with a bill for a number of unplayed, unpaid for features except as a result of his own actions.

Sections III and IV (a) are considerably weakened by an escape clause (sec. XII) which, depending on a number of eventualities, relieves the five major companies from these restrictions after August 31, 1942. In the first place, these sections will become inoperative if, before June 1, 1942, the three other defendants in the suit— Columbia, Universal, and United Artists—are not subject to similar conditions. If any different conditions are imposed on these three companies, any one of the five major companies may elect to observe similar restrictions, if it so desires.

Subdivision (g) of section XII assumes that all eight companies will have been brought under the decree by June 1, 1942, since these paragraphs only become operative after September 1, 1943. Subdivision (g) relieves the signatories from the trade showing and blocks-of-five provisions of the decree if 25 percent or more of the features released for exhibition in the United States are distributed by other means, or if 12½ percent or more of the total gross income from film rentals, excluding the gross income of States' right exchanges, is derived from pictures licensed otherwise than in accordance with sections III and IV (a).

Subdivision (h) goes into effect after September 1, 1942. After this date sections III and IV (a) become inoperative if the competition of those using methods of sale contrary to these provisions "has substantially and adversely affected" the business of any one of the consenting defendants.

Subdivision (g) and (h) together agree, in effect, that if the provisions with respect to block booking and blind selling are successful in permitting new competition to the major producers to develop, these companies will be free to return to these methods in order to stifle this new competition.

Finally, the signatories are released from the trade showing and blocks-of-five provisions of the decree if at any time an Act of Congress requiring trade showing or limiting the number of feature pictures which may be licensed in a block is passed. Considering all these avenues of escape, it seems improbable that these provisions will be in effect for a very long period of time.

FORCING OF SHORTS AND FOREIGNS

Section IV (b) of the consent decree states:

No distributor defendant shall require an exhibitor to license short subjects, newsreels, trailers, or serials (* * * collectively referred to as shorts) as a condition of licensing features. No distributor defendant shall require an exhibitor to license reissues, westerns, or foreigns (* * * collectively referred to as foreigns) as a condition of licensing other features.

On the surface this appears to be an unequivocal response to the exhibitors' complaint against forcing of shorts, news reels, serials or westerns. However, there is no requirement regarding the way in which such subjects shall be licensed. Presumably, sales will be made in as large a block as possible and at the beginning of a season. Features, on the other hand, will be almost necessarily sold throughout the year. There is no assurance that a distributor will view sympathetically the feature-picture requirements of an exhibitor who has failed to contract for short subjects.

Claims that licensing of features has been made conditional upon execution of a short subject contract may be arbitrated. But it will be a most difficult matter to relate the price paid for feature pictures during a season to a contract which may or may not have been entered into for short subjects at some previous time.

BUYING POWER

Section V is aimed at decentralization of circuit buying power, inasmuch as it requires a circuit with theaters in more than one exchange area to make individual contracts for its theaters in each district, and it requires that the contract in one area not be conditioned on a contract in another. However, circuit contracts can still be negotiated at the main office of the circuit.

It may be mentioned that an exchange area is not a small territory. Thirty-one exchange areas cover the entire United States. The buying power of all the theaters of a single circuit located in one exchange area is thus likely to be no small factor in contract negotiations. This provision, therefore, stops a long way short of requiring bargaining for films on a local basis.

EXCLUSIVE EXHIBITION RIGHTS

Section VI provides that no major distributor shall refuse to license pictures to an exhibitor on some run "upon terms and conditions fixed by the distributor which are not calculated to defeat the purpose of this section." The exhibitor must be able to "satisfy reasonable minimum standards of theater operation" and "be reputable and responsible." The provision is qualified in that the distributor may refuse to grant a run to an exhibitor if this "will have the effect of reducing the distributors total film revenue in the competitive area in which such exhibitor's theater is located." The burden of proof that granting such a run has reduced the distributor's total film revenue in the area rests on the distributor.

This provision is an attempt to answer exhibitors' charges that in some areas, independent theaters have been unable to operate in competition with circuit theaters because the major companies have refused to provide them with any pictures. The distributors' answer to this charge has been that pictures have been refused only when operation of an additional theater was uneconomical and tended to reduce their entire revenue from the area. It will be noted that in the actual application of this provision, the prospective exhibitor must be prepared to bid more than the difference between the circuit's offer for exclusive exhibition rights and for first-run privileges only, since relief is subject to the condition that the distributor's total revenue be not reduced.

CLEARANCE

Section VIII of the decree provides that—

Controversies arising upon the complaint of an exhibitor that the clearance applicable to his theater is unreasonable shall be subject to arbitration under the following provisions:

It is recognized that clearance, reasonable as to time and area, is essential the distribution and exhibition of motion pictures.

In determining whether any clearance complained of is unreasonable, the arbitrator shall take into consideration the following factors and accord to them the importance and weight to which each is entitled, regardless of the order in which they are listed:

(1) The historical development of clearance in the particular area wherein the theaters involved are located; (2) The admission prices of the theaters involved; (3) The character and location of the theaters involved, including size, type of entertainment, appointments, transit facilities, etc.; (4) The policy of the theaters involved, such as the showing of double features, gift nights, give-aways, premiums, cut rate tickets, lotteries, etc.; (5) The rental terms and license fees paid by the theaters involved and the revenues derived by the distributor defendant from such theaters; (6) The extent to which the theaters involved compete with each other for patronage; and (7) All other business considerations, except that the arbitrator shall disregard the fact that a theater involved is affiliated with a distributor or with a circuit of theaters.

When an arbitration proceeding is instituted, the arbitrator must first decide if clearance is unreasonable. If his decision is in the affirmative, he is then empowered to fix the maximum clearance period which may be granted in subsequent licensing agreements.

The clearance granted by a distributor to theaters in which he has a financial interest is not subject to arbitration. Clearance on so-called "specials" which includes pictures which may be roadshown at advanced prices is also exempted from arbitration.

Any distributor or exhibitor affected by an arbitration award may institute new proceedings at any time on the grounds that conditions have changed so as to require modification of the original award.

This provision represents a very real·concession to exhibitors who have complained of unfair clearance restrictions. It probably reflects an opinion by the major companies that their long run interest is best served by equitable clearance schedules.

·WITHHOLDING DELIVERY OF PRINTS

Section IX of the decree provides that distributors shall not withhold from an exhibitor delivery of prints available in its exchange in order to give a competing exhibitor a prior playing date not provided for in his license. A strict interpretation of this provision would indicate that it applied only as between two exhibitors playing on the same run. It would not apply, for example, to delay in delivery to give a prior-run exhibitor a longer clearance period. Whether this strict interpretation was intended or whether it will be adopted is uncertain.

RUN

Section X provides that:

Controversies arising upon a complaint by an independent exhibitor that a distributor defendant has arbitrarily refused to license its features for exhibition on the run requested by said exhibitor * * * shall be subject to arbitration.

This provision is hemmed about with so many restrictions as immediately to limit its application to a very small number of cases. In many situations it will be meaningless.

In the first place, it applies only to theaters which were in existence or which replaced a theater in existence on the day the decree was entered—November 20, 1940. Secondly, complaints may be entered only by independent exhibitors who are defined in this case as exhibitors "wholly independent of any circuit of more than five theaters." Beyond these restrictions, it is expressly stipulated that no arbitration award shall be entered unless:

The distributor refused to license pictures on the run requested for a period of not less than 3 successive months; the run desired was enjoyed by a circuit theater (a circuit is defined as consisting of not less than 15 theaters); features sufficient in nature and quantity to enable the complainant's theater to operate on the run requested were not available; the complainant operated his theater on the same run or an earlier run than the one requested between July 20, 1935, and July 20, 1940, or subsequent to July 20, 1940, and during the two consecutive motion-picture seasons immediately preceding the complaint the complainant operated his theater on the same run as or on an earlier run than that enjoyed by the circuit theater and during such period exhibited substantially all the features released during the period by the distributor, or subsequent to July 20, 1935, and prior to July 20, 1940, the complainant demanded from the distributor the particular run or an earlier run, in writing, or filed a similar complaint with a local clearance and zoning board under the N. R. A. which was not disposed of by administrative decision under the code prior to May 27, 1935 (a similar complaint by a prior operator of a theater is acceptable provided the present complainant operated the theater specified for. at least 1 year prior to the entry of the decree); and finally refusal to license pictures on the run requested by the complainant was in fact because the run had been given to a circuit theater.

After listing all these preliminary restrictions on the exact character of the exhibitor who may be entitled to file a complaint, the consent decree goes on to list those factors which should be taken into account by the arbitrator in making his award. These are the usual considerations which one might expect would wholly determine the playing position of a theater. The many restrictions listed would appear to serve no useful purpose beyond one of limiting the exhibitors who might request proceedings to improve their run.

Finally, if the arbitrator decides that a complaint is justified, he may enter an award against the distributor, but this does not guarantee any improvement over past procedure. The award simply requires that in the future the distributor shall not license pictures to the circuit theater on the run in question unless the contract or agreement is separate and not a part of any contract or agreement for the licensing of features in any other theater. This, of course, does not guarantee that the complainant will get the run he desires.

After a final award has been made, the complainant is permitted to file another arbitration proceeding on the grounds that "such award has not been complied with in good faith by the distributor against whom it was entered." If the arbitrator in this proceeding finds that the distributor has failed to comply with the previous award, the arbitrator may award compensatory damages to the complaining exhibitor for any loss he has suffered because of the distributor's failure to comply with the original award. This new arbitration proceeding must be instituted within 60 days after the alleged violation has occurred, and the damages which may be awarded can apply only to losses in the 60-day period.

The extremely careful restrictions with which the possibility of arbitration of run has been hedged about contrast most curiously with the forthright treatment accorded arbitration of clearance. In this connection, it may be recalled that most of the affiliated-theater interests are in prior runs. Since some clearance must always exist between runs (it is recognized in section VIII that "clearance reasonable as to time and area is essential in the distribution and exhibition of motion pictures"), it appears that the affiliated interests were willing to make some concessions with respect to clearance, but were most reluctant to admit the possibility of any widespread disturbance of their control of the profitable prior runs.

FURTHER ACQUISITION OF THEATERS

As stated earlier in this appendix, one of the declared objectives of the antitrust suit filed against the major companies was to compel them to divest themselves of their theater holdings. The consent decree makes no such proposal; instead in section XI it provides that:

For a period of 3 years after the entry of the decree herein each of the consenting defendants will notify the Department of Justice immediately of any legally binding commitment for the acquisition by it of any additional theater or theaters.

During such period each such defendant will also report to the Department of Justice * * * the changes in its theater position, if any * * * as follows, together with a statement of the reasons for such changes.

(a) Theaters contracted to be built, or under construction; (b) theaters lost or disposed of; (c) theaters acquired; (d) interests in theaters acquired, with a statement of the nature and extent of such interests.

* * * For a period of 3 years following the entry of this decree, no consenting defendant shall enter upon a general program of expanding its theater holdings. Nothing herein shall prevent any such defendant from acquiring theaters or interests therein to protect its investment or its competitive position or for ordinary purposes of its business.

This last provision, requiring a decision as to whether one of the defendants has acquired a theater "for ordinary purposes of its business," or for some other purpose, renders the whole provision vague if not meaningless.

Proceedings based on a violation of this subdivision * * * shall be only by application to the Court for injunctive relief against the consenting defendant complained against, which shall be limited to restraining the acquisition, or ordering the divestiture, of the theaters or interests therein, if any, about to be acquired, or acquired, in violation of this section.

ARBITRATION

The decree deals with a number of points of friction which have arisen between the major companies and independent exhibitors. In most of these cases arbitration of any disputes is stipulated. Accordingly, the decree sets up elaborate arbitration machinery. The American Arbitration Association is appointed administrator of the arbitration system. The association is required to set up a panel of not less than 10 impartial arbitrators and a clerk in each city in which 3 or more of the defendants maintain exchanges.

Elaborate and detailed rules of arbitration are given. In any case subject to arbitration, proceedings may be instituted by filing a demand accompanied by a fee of $10 with the appropriate local arbitration tribunal. Each party in an arbitration proceeding must deposit for every day or part of a day that the hearing lasts an amount equal to the arbitrator's per diem fee which is not to exceed $50 per day. The expenses are to be paid by the party against whom the award is made. Extensive powers are awarded the arbitrator to insure the attendance of witnesses, to examine books and records, and to secure such information as he may deem necessary to guide him in making a decision.

An appeals board is to be set up consisting of three members of "known impartiality and distinction" to be appointed by the court. The decision of any arbitration proceeding may be taken to the appeals board by filing with the local secretary a fee of $25 and three copies of the record of the arbitration hearing. The cost of obtaining the record must be borne by the appellant.

The arbitration system is to be financed in part by the filing fees and expenses collected in the arbitration hearings. The principal burden of the system, however, will be shouldered by the five major companies. Each of these will be assessed proportionately to their annual gross receipts from film rentals. The budget for the first year is set at not more than $490,000.

All provisions of the consent decree dealing with trade practices are to be enforced solely through arbitration proceedings instituted by an injured party. Only in the case of a general program of theater acquisition in violation of the decree is it provided that reference will be taken directly to the court. In this case the Department of Justice, is limited to a request for injunctive relief to consist of an order prohibiting the acquisition of particular theaters or divestiture if an agreement has been consummated.

The defendant companies and their agents in section II are enjoined from violating any of the provisions of the degree. However, section XVI states:

. No consenting defendant and no officer, director, agent or employee of any such defendant, shall be deemed to have violated any provision of this decree if the arbitration of disputes or controversies arising relative to the subject matter thereof is herein provided for, unless such defendant has refused to arbitrate such a dispute or controversy in the manner and under the conditions specified in this decree and in the Rules of Arbitration and Appeals which are filed herewith, as amended from time to time, or has failed or refused to abide by and perform the final award made and entered in such an arbitration proceeding.

Thus, while the consenting defendants are prohibited from certain actions by one part of the decree, a second section permits them to continue these practices unless in a particular instance they refuse to submit to arbitration or to abide by an award following arbitration.

Ordinarily, enforcement of a consent decree is assumed by the Department of Justice. When the Department feels that a provision of a decree has been violated, the Department can ask that the violator be adjudged in contempt of court and request that an appropriate penalty be imposed. It appears that in this case the Department has specifically resigned these powers. Enforcement of the decree is instead imposed on the members of the industry and to a considerable extent on the weaker members of the industry.

It is true that the fee required to file a case is not large. However, the necessity of depositing each day an amount equal to the per diem expense of the arbitration proceeding may impose a real financial burden on the small exhibitor; a not inconsiderable sum may be involved if extended hearings are required. Moreover, the provision that the loser in an arbitration proceeding must pay for the expenses of the hearing will certainly tend to discourage any smaller members of the industry from filing a complaint of doubtful validity, and some element of risk will always be involved.

Moreover, any award may be appealed by either of the parties to the appeals board which may at its option order oral hearings. The appeals board will be located in New York City, and hearings will be held only in that place. The expense of defending an appeal may thus be not inconsiderable.

The extent to which the various provisions of the decree will be enforced thus depends to some extent on the willingness of small exhibitors to risk amounts of money which to them may be relatively quite important. And in many cases the financial gain to be expected even from a favorable award may be quite small.

In connection with enforcement of the decree through arbitration proceedings, it may be noted that the power of the arbitrator in making awards is quite limited. In most cases the arbitrator can do no more than find that a provision of the decree has been violated and require that the violator discontinue the practice. In only two cases is the arbitrator empowered to impose a fine on a distributor violating the decree, and this fine in either case is not to exceed the sum of $500. Fines may be imposed where a distributor has made the sale of features contingent upon the sale of short subjects or foreigns or other features, and where the buying power of a circuit in more than one exchange area has been considered by the distributor in film negotiations.

In only one case can the arbitrator award damages to an exhibitor and then only to the extent that the exhibitor can prove financial loss during a 60-day period by reason of the distributor's failure to comply with the previous award. In most cases, then, the distributor in continuing a practice in violation of the decree has only to fear financial loss to the extent of the expenses of an arbitration hearing. In no case can he be faced by contempt proceedings in a Federal court.

On the other hand, the contempt procedure method of enforcement of a consent decree is time-consuming and sometimes awkward and expensive. The application of this method to the enforcement of a decree affecting many thousands of transactions occurring in every part of the United States each year might prove wholly unsatisfactory. The limited resources and personnel available to the Department of Justice for work of this character is not to be ignored. Moreover, the record of the contempt procedure method as a device for securing enforcement of a consent decree is not wholly impressive.[5] There is thus room for argument that as between enforcement of the decree by contempt procedure or by arbitration, the latter, while it leaves much to be desired, is to be preferred.

---

[5] Cf. Temporary National Economic Committee, Monograph 16, pp. 88-97.

INDEX

INDEX

90INDEX